BRITISH AND AMERICAN ACES OF WORLD WAR I

BRITISH AND AMERICAN ACES OF WORLD WAR I

THE PICTORIAL RECORD

Norman Franks

Schiffer Military History
Atglen, PA

Book design by Robert Biondi.

Library of Congress Catalog Number: 2005924633.

Printed in China.
ISBN: 0-7643-2341-5

Published by Schiffer Publishing Ltd.
4880 Lower Valley Road
Atglen, PA 19310
Phone: (610) 593-1777
FAX: (610) 593-2002
E-mail: Info@schifferbooks.com.
Visit our web site at: www.schifferbooks.com
Please write for a free catalog.
This book may be purchased from the publisher.
Please include $3.95 postage.
Try your bookstore first.

In Europe, Schiffer books are distributed by:
Bushwood Books
6 Marksbury Ave.
Kew Gardens
Surrey TW9 4JF
England
Phone: 44 (0)20 8392-8585
FAX: 44 (0)20 8392-9876
E-mail: Bushwd@aol.com.
Free postage in the UK. Europe: air mail at cost.
Try your bookstore first.

INTRODUCTION

Once well on the way to producing *German Aces of World War I: The Pictorial Record* it seemed logical to suggest to the Schiffer Publishing Company that a companion volume should be published, covering the World War I aces of the British Empire and Commonwealth, plus the American aces of that war.

The immediate problem was that while the German aces numbered a little over 400, the British and Americans combined ranged in the region of 900. Quite apart from the size of the problem, the second worry was that it would be an almost impossible task to try to collect together reasonable portraits or just pictures of many of the lower scoring aces. It was therefore decided that I would concentrate on those British aces that achieved ten or more victories.

With the Americans, who served both with the British Royal Flying Corps, Royal Naval Air Service or – after 1 April 1918 – the Royal Air Force, and the U.S. Air Service, it was less of a problem for my collection included well over 80 of the 100 or so aces and I felt sure some of the gaps would be filled before the book was ready for the publisher. Therefore, while the British aces only include those of ten plus victory claims, the American section covers all, from Rickenbacker's 26 down to Robert Todd's five.

This means, of course, that those Americans who only served with the British and are generally listed in so-called 'ace lists' of World War I British aces, I have extracted from that list and have lumped them all together in this American section. The book's indexes (alpha ace lists) however, will show all aces in strict alphabetical order, be they British, Commonwealth, or American.

It should be emphasised that this book contains just the *fighter* aces, not pilots, observers or gunners who were given ace status by virtue of claiming, or being credited with, five victories. Those men can be found in books with which I am associated: *Above the Trenches*, (with Chris Shores and Russell Guest) *Over the Front*, (with F.W. Bailey) and *Above the War Fronts*, (with Russell Guest and Gregory Alegi) all published by Grub Street, London.

• • •

One might wonder why there were so many British and American aces compared to German aces. Quite apart from the fact that by 1918 at least there were more British and American fighter pilots serving in France or Italy than there were German, the system of scoring – or victory credits – were very different. This led to the Allied pilots being able to be credited with more victories, thereby expanding those eligible to be termed 'aces'.

To explain this is both complicated but simple! By 1915 the air war was starting to become serious and pilots of both sides soon began to develop methods of attacking each other. With the coming of the Fokker *Eindecker*, which began to carry a machine gun that could fire through the whirling blades of the propeller, the advantage was firmly on the German side. Numbers, however, were of necessity, small, and these Fokker monoplanes had to be spread out amongst German units along the whole of the Western Front. This smallness in numbers and the need to keep secret the aeroplane's machine gun interrupter gear, led to the German fighter pilots flying a defensive war, and thus their air fighters were not permitted to cross the trenches – the lines – that ran from the Channel coast to the Swiss border.

On the other hand, the British and French airmen, but particularly the British, were positively encouraged to take the air war to the Germans, and so daily their aircraft crossed the lines in order to do battle with the dreaded Hun. Once it was deemed something of note to record the number of hostile aircraft a particular pilot managed to bring down, whether Allied or German, it followed that some sort of confirmation system needed to be put in place, so that the various headquarters could allow a victory credit to be given.

On the German side, with the majority of air fights happening above their side of the lines, it was possible to view wreckage of aircraft brought down, capture airmen who had been forced to land or crash land in their occupied territory, or – more gruesomely – have dead bodies to aid confirmation. The German system therefore developed into confirmations where there was no doubt that an Allied machine had been destroyed or captured, simply because there was tangible evidence. Where the German system got bogged down was where an Allied aeroplane managed to go down – or appear to go down – on the Allied side.

These were no occasional events – they happened almost daily. German pilots, keen to have a victory confirmed, were naturally eager for unit adjutants to enquire of front line troops or observers if they had seen such-and-such an aeroplane go down above a certain sector of the line or near a named wood or devastated village, etc. This became something of a grey area as can be imagined. Not all front-line soldiers cared a jot whether some air hero who was at that moment sipping coffee in the safety of his mess some miles behind the front lines, had a claim confirmed or not. They might say, yes, they had seen an aeroplane go down, and it looked as if it crashed, but they were no experts in either aircraft recognition, or how an aeroplane might look if it was about to crash into matchwood, or simply land and then be towed away, or even take off later.

Sometimes of course, the downed aircraft could be seen, standing in a field or nosed over in a shell hole beyond the front line trenches. If this was the case then it was generally shelled by artillery and blasted to pieces, which was a positive way of saying it was destroyed and could, therefore, be legitimised as a victory. Yet some confirmations were given where we now know that the aeroplane did not in fact crash, didn't even come down, its pilot simply scooted for home so low that his escape went unobserved.

Mist, low cloud or trees and small hills, caused many such problems. Nevertheless, due to the vagaries involved, sometimes a victory was confirmed whereas in fact no aeroplane had even been damaged, let alone lost.

On the Allied side, once these things became important (to the aviators anyway), one can see that to gain confirmation of a destroyed opponent became more problematical with the fighting being often well beyond the lines and out of sight of any Allied front line unit that might be looking eastwards. For one thing, if a battle was raging, soldiers and observers would have their heads well down below the parapets. Exploding shells, machine gun fire and snipers didn't encourage anyone to stand around looking at aeroplanes several miles away. Blinding sun, clouds, mist and ground fog, not to mention gun-smoke, also made observations difficult.

A British pilot returning to his base and claiming a victory needed to have some kind of confirmation, either from brother pilots in the fight, or pilots and observers from other squadrons, or from soldiers on the ground who did happen to see what was happening. Both sides, of course, in an air fight where it seemed an adversary was getting the better of the situation, had simply to spin away earthwards, knowing that most experienced fighter pilots would not follow them down for fear of an attack themselves. Once down and out of the immediate danger area, the pilot would come out of his spin, fly home, and tell his chums how lucky he had been. A change of trousers perhaps adding an emphasis to his recent experience!

Meantime, the British pilot was landing at his base and claiming what he deemed to be a German machine going down 'out of control' and undoubtedly smashed itself into the French or Belgian countryside. These *out of control* victory claims were the norm of the day, and while no doubt the majority were simply pilots getting out of trouble, they were often classed as 'out of control' (meaning that they probably crashed), while in reality they were no more than a 'possible'.

The French, of course, deemed these claims as 'probables' and did not add them to a pilot's official score, whereas the British recorded them as 'victories' and did add them to a pilot's tally. So, whereas a Frenchman with claims of six destroyed and three probables only had a score of six, a British pilot could boast a score of nine!

Another vagary of different systems was that while German pilots did not share victories, Allied pilots did. If two or more German pilots got into a fight and each thought his fire had crippled the opponent, only one victory credit would be awarded. That would go to either the man who persuaded his CO that he had caused to enemy plane to crash or burn, or a gentlemanly toss of a coin or throw of a dice decided, otherwise it went to arbitration where a decision by a third party was final.

The British, French and later the American Air Service, who in any event operated alongside the French and used their systems, shared victories. In some units anything up to half a dozen pilots could each record part of a claim, but in a man's score each 'bit' was recorded as 'one' victory. Therefore, a pilot could – and did - share in five victories and become an ace without ever having brought down a single opponent on his own. Just to add to the confusion, an American who fought only with the British, scored victories as per their system, whereas Americans with the French could not count 'probables'. David Putnam, as an example, scored just 13 victories but had more than 15 probables; ie. 28 under British rules. But these were the systems in vogue; the ones accepted and used.

When I first began to study World War I air fighting, I initially thought that the system of counting scores were just the same as World War II, which I had studied first that being nearer to my age.

Thus I knew that someone like Johnnie Johnson, had been credited with 38 victories (including shares), but I also knew he had quite a number of probables and damaged, which did not alter his 'destroyed' tally. So, once I started to read of pilots such as, say, Keith Caldwell, I assumed his score of 25 meant 25 destroyed. It was only when I began to research more deeply, that I discovered that in his case (as in all others) his 25 was made up of 13 destroyed (including two shared), one captured (ie: brought down on the Allied side of the lines), and 11 out of control (ie: what the French deemed to be probables). So had be been a Frenchman, his score would have been 14.

Over recent years this 'out of control' business has produced any number of criticisms from historians and researchers, some of whom have been trying to re-vamp the aces scores by counting only those enemy aircraft deemed – or credited – as being destroyed. While this may be an interesting exercise for them, it misses the point. That point being that while hindsight is a marvellous thing and one can discover that certain aircraft claimed were not destroyed, the system used at the time cannot be partially ignored and reconstituted in another form.

The main stumbling block, it seems to me, is in the word *victory*. In World War I air fighting was just starting, and even though one might argue that the system of victory credits had its faults by today's standards, it was nevertheless, the system OF THE TIME. Again, in the early days, 'victories' were interpreted as just that, a victory over an opponent. In 1915-1916, a German pilot, finding himself in trouble, or wounded, or his aircraft damaged, was inclined to land as soon as possible, in order to get out of trouble, to seek medical help, or before his machine fell apart. Most British airmen would leave it at that, leave the German alone and fly off feeling he had achieved something positive. In those early days it was too un-gentlemanly to dive down and strafe the downed machine, pilot and or crew. That later changed as the war became more deadly, but at first the victorious British pilot had done a good job.

He may not have killed an enemy or destroyed his aircraft, but he had stopped that enemy from carrying out his assigned task. That task could have been any number of jobs, each designed to bring death and destruction to the Allied side. He may have been directing German artillery onto British soldiers; he may have been taking photographs of positions that might later be shelled or bombed; he might have been himself on a bombing sortie. To have made that German abort his mission was a victory of sorts, which is why some of the early aces had 'forced to land' victories in their scores. Only later were these not counted. The mute point here is that a mortally wounded pilot who succeeds in landing, becomes just as dead as one spinning in from 15,000 feet. Yet one may become a victory, the other does not.

All sides also included the destruction of observation balloons in their scores, although again, the sharing system only worked for the Allied side. Oddly enough though, the balloon had to be seen to be destroyed – i.e.: burning. A balloon suspected of only being holed, even if seen well deflated, was not credited. And again talking brutally, a dead observer was not a victory unless his balloon burned.

To sum up. World War I pilots achieved victories of several categories. World War II pilots achieved victories but only destroyed claims – if confirmed – were counted in scores.

• • •

Something else needs to be explained for the layman or embryo aviation historian, and that concerns two-seater fighters. These are the machines that carried a pilot and an observer, the latter handling one or two machine-guns in addition to any his pilot might control. The two main types which produced 'fighter' aces were the FE2b / FE2d 'pusher' two-seater (the engine faced the rear and pushed the machine through the air) and the BF2b – the famed Bristol Fighter.

Both types were formidable fighting machines, especially with an expert and daring crew. Both were agile and its crew could fire both forwards and rearwards, and of course, in a 90 degree arc from the rear gunner position. The pilot was able to concentrate on attacking opponents knowing his observer/gunner was watching their tail. One odd thing about these two seater crews as regards scores of victories, is that if a pilot had claimed five victories and his observer five, the pilot was deemed to have ten victories, while the observer only had his five!

There are a number of FE2 and BF2b pilot aces portrayed in this book and their scores are the combined total they and their observer or observers claimed.

• • •

The aces depicted in this pictorial record are fighter pilots. While some so-called ace lists have, over the years, noted ace pilots and some ace observers, this book, as I mentioned earlier, only portrays photographs of fighter pilot aces. They do not include observers, pilots of Corps or bomber squadrons, just fighter pilots.

As with *German Aces of World War I: The Pictorial Record*, I only show name, rank, unit(s) score and where known, dates and places of birth, and death. Fuller biographies of all these aces can, as most serious historians will know, can be found in several of my co-authored books on World War I aces (for this book *Above the Trenches* in particular).

It is not always possible to absolutely sure of a pilot's place of birth. Records that can be viewed today may give a place of birth very different from a place of residence when that man joined the forces. His family could have moved, for example, or he was born in a foreign country, but soon came to his native country to live and be brought up. Or he could have married and set up home away from the area of his birth. Therefore, where a town or city is mentioned, while it could have been where he was born, it can only be fairly certain that it is where he came from once the war started and he joined the colours.

The vast majority of pilots joined the Royal Flying Corps, Royal Naval Air Service or Royal Air Force, came from many varied regiments or commands. These have been noted for interest, but please bear in mind that these units are not necessarily the only one a man may have served with. Those mentioned are the units in which they were serving, or perhaps been commissioned into, at the time they transferred to aviation.

Where an army unit is not shown it generally means he joined the flying services direct but while this is a rule of thumb, it cannot always be relied on to be correct. Many Canadians, for instance, who served in the RNAS, joined direct in Canada, while others joined directly into the RFC. Americans in the USAS generally tended to join their air service direct too, the route being to join the Aviation Section of the U.S. Signal Corps. Americans with the British either joined the RFC in Canada before the U.S. came into the war, or were USAS officers attached to the RFC/RAF for combat experience. Many other Americans joined the French air force as volunteers prior to the U.S. came into the war, mainly via the Foreign Legion and then the Lafayette Flying Corps.

• • •

When ace lists began to appear in the 1920s and 1930s, pilot's victory scores were collected by enthusiasts from magazines or from reading citations from medal awards that were printed in various editions of the *London Gazette*, then listed. Very little came from official sources, therefore these lists were not very accurate. It was not until Chris Shores, Russell Guest and I produced the book *Above the Trenches* that a more definitive and more accurate listing of British and Commonwealth aces became available. While this has been slightly amended, including additions in our Supplement to *ATT*, the overall list has remained the same and largely been unchallenged.

However, I had a slight problem when starting this book as to which ace to begin with. When Taffy Jones published his biography on Mick Mannock, for reasons which are now more understood, he chose to record Mannock's score as 73 and it has been this score that generally tops any published list of British World War I aces. In *ATT* we more or less established that his true score was something in the region of 61. For reasons that many World War I aviation historians will understand, I have decided to keep his name at the top of the list. While it can be established that a number of World War I aces did not score the victories they have hitherto been acknowledged to have scored, I have, by the same token, kept the list in more or less that form which is understood by the general historian or interested party.

ACKNOWLEDGMENTS

I am grateful to the Schiffer Company for allowing me to indulge still further my interest in World War I aviation and in particular to the scout pilots of Britain, her then Empire, and those Americans who fought alongside them or in their own air service.

Over many years of interest I have gradually collected scores of photographs of men and machines but had still to rely on a number of friends and colleagues to help fill the gaps. In particular I have to thank Frank Cheesman whose archives have to be among the best, and I am very grateful to him for making many of the rarer photos available to me. Also to Mike O'Connor, Stuart Leslie, Tony Mellor-Ellis, Mike Westrop, Jim Brown, John Grech, Barry Gray and Michael Partridge.

Each and every one of them have my grateful thanks. Without them this book would be the poorer. It would have been nice to have gathered 100% of the faces needed, but no doubt some of the missing will turn up after publication. This is good, for any further editions may then be updated to include these missing portraits. I would welcome any additional pictures or information, especially about their fates.

As with *German Aces of World War I* the photographic quality varies greatly. All these pictures are over 80 years old, and few are original prints, these having been copied and re-copied over the years. None of the original photographers are still alive but we today are grateful for their professional or non-professional work in preserving these wartime portraits, whether taken in a studio or as a snapshot on a windy airfield. Dozens of historians have their own collections and I have been grateful to many for letting me have copies to add to my own collection.

Norman Franks
East Sussex, England

Abbreviations

AFC	Air Force Cross
AFC	Australian Flying Corps
CdG(B)	Croix de Guerre (Belgium)
CdG(F)	Croix de Guerre (French)
DCM	Distinguished Conduct Medal
DFC	Distinguished Flying Cross (British flying award also awarded to American pilots)
DOAS	Died on Active Service
DoI	Died of Injuries
DoW	Died of Wounds
DSC	Distinguished Service Cross (RNAS – British award) (USAS – US award)
DSM	Distinguished Service Medal
DSO	Distinguished Service Order
HD	Home Defence
KIA	Killed in Action
KIFA	Killed in Flying Accident
KOAS	Killed on Active Service
LdH	Légion d'Honneur
MC	Military Cross
Md'A	Medaglia d'Argento al Valor Militare
MM	Military Medal
MM(F)	Medaille Militaire (French)
MoH	Medal of Honour (USA)
OLC	Oak Leaf Clusters (USA) (equivalent of British Bars)
RNAS	Royal Naval Air Service
Sqn	Squadron
VC	Victoria Cross
*	First Bar
**	Second Bar

THE PICTORIAL RECORD

Major Edward Mannock
VC DSO* MC*
Born Brighton, Sussex, 21 May 1888. KIA France, 26 July 1918
Royal Engineers; 40, 74 & 85 Squadrons
73 victories

Lieutenant-Colonel William Avery Bishop
VC DSO* MC DFC LdH(F) CdG(F)
Born Owen Sound, Ontario Canada, 8 February 1894.
Died Palm Springs, USA, 11 September 1956
Canadian Mounted Rifles; 21, 60 & 85 Squadrons
72 victories
(on the left is L.K. Callahan (5) USAS)

Lt-Colonel Raymond Collishaw
DSO* DSC DFC
Born Nanaimo, British Columbia, 22 November 1893.
Died West Vancouver, 28 September 1976
3 Wing, 3 Sqn, 10 Sqn, 13 Sqn RNAS, 203 & 47 Squadrons RAF
61 victories

Major James Thomas Byford McCudden
VC DSO* MC* MM CdG(F)
Born Gillingham, Kent, 28 March 1895. KIFA France, 9 July 1918
Royal Engineers; 3, 20, 29, 56 & 60 Squadrons
57 victories

Captain Anthony Frederick Weatherby Beauchamp Proctor
VC DSO MC* DFC
Born Mosal Bay, South Africa, 4 September 1894. KIFA Enford, nr Netheravon, 21 June 1921
84 Squadron
54 victories

Major Donald Roderick MacLaren
DSO MC* DFC LdH(F) CdG(F)
Born Ottawa, Canada, 28 May 1893. Died July 1989
46 Squadron
54 victories
(In the picture MacLaren is standing in front of his Sopwith Camel)

Major William George Barker
VC DSO* MC** CdG Md'A
Born Dauphin, Manitoba, 3 November 1894. KIFA Rockliffe, 12 March 1930
Canadian Mounted Rifles; 9, 4, 15, 28, 66, 139, 201 Squadrons
50 victories

Captain Robert Alexander Little
DSO* DSC*
Born Melbourne, Australia, 19 July 1895. KIA France, 27 May 1918
1 Wing, 8 Sqn RNAS, 203 Sqn RAF
47 victories

Captain George Edward Henry McElroy
MC** DFC*
Born Donnybrook, Dublin, 14 May 1893. KIA France, 31 July 1918
Royal Irish Regt; 40 & 24 Squadrons
46 victories

Captain Albert Ball
VC DSO** MC, Order of St George 4th Class
Born Nottingham, 14 August 1896. KIA France, 7 May 1917
2/7 Sherwood Foresters; 13, 11, 8, 60 & 56 Squadrons
44 victories

Major Tom Falcon Hazell
DSO MC DFC*
Born Clifden, Galway, 7 August 1892. Died Newport, Co Mayo, Ireland, 4 Sep 1946
7/Royal Irish Rifles; 1, 24 & 203 Squadrons
43 victories

Captain Philip Fletcher Fullard
DSO MC*
Born Hatfield, 27 June 1897. Died 24 April 1984
Royal Fusiliers; 1 Squadron
40 victories

Major John Ingles Gilmour
DSO MC**
Born Helensburgh, Scotland, 28 June 1896. Died 1928
Argyll & Sutherland Highlanders; 27, 65 & 28 Squadrons
39 victories

Captain William Lancelot Jordan
DSC* DFC
From London, born Georgetown, SA, 3 December 1896. Died (car accident) 1930s
8 Sqn RNAS, 208 Sqn RAF
39 victories

Captain Alfred Clayburn Atkey
MC*
From Minebow, Saskatchewan, born 16 August 1894. Died Toronto, 10 February 1971
18 & 22 Squadrons
38 victories
(picture shows Atkey sitting, with C.G. Gass MC, one of his observers)

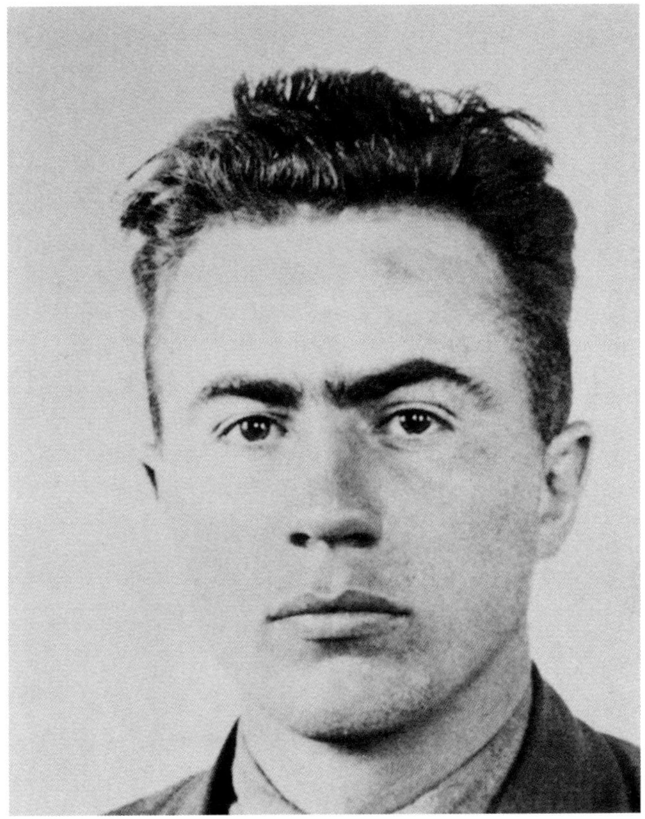

Captain William Gordon Claxton
DSO DFC
Born Gladstone, Manitoba, 1 June 1899. Died Toronto, 28 September 1967
41 Squadron
37 victories

Captain James Ira Thomas Jones
DSO MC DFC*
Born St Clears, S Wales, 18 April 1896. Died Glamorgan, 30 August 1960
10 & 74 Squadrons
37 victories

Captain Joseph Stewart Temple Fall
DSC** AFC
From Hillbank, Vancouver Island, born 17 November 1895.
Died Enderby, BC, 1 December 1988
3 Sqn & 9 Sqn RNAS
36 victories

Captain Samuel Marcus Kinkead
DSO DSC* DFC*
From Johannesburg, SA, born 25 February 1897. KIFA, The Solant, 12 March 1928
3 Wing, 1 Sqn RNAS, 210 & 47 Squadrons RAF
35 victories (inc 3 in N Russia 1919)

Captain Frederick Robert Gordon McCall
DSO MC* DFC
Born Vernon BC, 4 December 1896. Died 2 January 1949
Alberta Rgt; 13 & 41 Squadrons
35 victories
(In the picture McCall is sitting in an SE5A)

Captain Henry Winslow Woollett
DSO MC* LdH(F) CdG
From Southwold, Suffolk, born 5 August 1895. Died 31 October 1969
Lincolnshire Rgt; 24 & 43 Squadrons
35 victories
(In the picture Woolett is seated in his Sopwith Camel)

Captain Francis Grainger Quigley
DSO MC*
Born Toronto, 10 July 1894. Died (influenza) Liverpool, 20 October 1918
Canadian Engineers; 70 Squadron
33 victories

Major Gerald Hilton Bowman
DSO MC* DFC CdG(B)
Born Manchester, 2 May 1891. Died 25 March 1970
3rd Royal Warwickshire Rgt; 26, 56 & 41 Squadrons
32 victories
(In the picture Bowman is sitting on the wheel of a captured Fokker DVII)

Major Rodric Stanley Dallas
DSO DSC* CdG(F)
Born Mount Stanley, Queensland, 30 July 1891. KIA France, 1 June 1918
Australian Army; 1 Wing, 1 Sqn RNAS, 40 Sqn RAF
32 victories

Andrew Edward McKeever
DSO MC* CdG
Born Listowel, Ontario, 21 August 1894. DoI (car accident) Ontario, 25 December 1919
58th Battn, CEF; 11 Squadron
31 victories

Captain Samuel Frederick Henry Thompson (NO PHOTO)
MC DFC
From Blackheath, SE London, born 30 August 1890. KIA France, 27 September 1918
Army Service Corps; 20 & 22 Squadrons
30 victories

Major Charles Dawson Booker
DSC CdG
Born Speldhurst, Kent, 21 April 1897. KIA France, 13 August 1918
5 Wing, 8 Sqn, 1 Sqn RNAS, 201 Sqn RAF
29 victories

Captain Percy Jack Clayson
MC DFC
Born Croydon, Surrey, 7 June 1896.
Royal Naval Air Service; 1 Squadron RFC/RAF
29 victories

Captain Arthur Henry Cobby
DSO DFC**
Born Melbourne, 26 August 1894. Died 11 November 1955
71 Sqn RFC, 4 Sqn AFC
29 victories
(In the picture Cobby is standing in front of an Avro 504)

Captain Leonard Henry Rochford
DSC* DFC
Born Enfield, 10 November 1896. Died 17 December 1986
3 Sqn RNAS, 203 Sqn RAF
29 victories
(In the picture Titch Rochford is standing in front of a Camel)

Major Albert Desbrisay Carter
DSO* CdG(B)
From Pointe de Bute, New Brunswick, born 2 June 1892.
KIFA nr Shoreham, England, 22 May 1919
Canadian infantry; 19 Squadron
28 victories

Captain John Everard Gurdon
DFC*
Born Balham, South London, 24 May 1898. Died Alassio, Italy, 14 April 1973
Suffolk Rgt; 22 Squadron
28 victories

Captain Reginald Theodore Carlos Hoidge
MC*
Born Toronto, 28 July 1894. Died New York City, 1 March 1963
Canadian Royal Garrison Artillery; 56 & 1 Squadrons
28 victories
(In the picture Hoidge is sitting in an early SE5)

Captain Dennis Latimer
MC DFC
Born Towyn, Merioneth, 31 August 1895.
20 Squadron
28 victories
(The picture shows Latimer at extreme left with comrades of 20 Squadron. To his left is W. Noble (Obs), P. Iaccaci (P), unknown, T.P. Middleton (P))

Captain Thomas Percy Middleton
DFC
Born Kew, South London, 10 May 1893.
6 London Bde; 48 & 20 Squadrons
28 victories

Captain Clifford Mackay McEwen
MC DFC, Italian Bronze Medal
Born Griswold, Manitoba, 2 July 1897. Died in Toronto, 6 August 1967
Canadian Army; 28 Squadron
27 victories
(In the picture McEwen is on the right, Lt Norman Cyril Jones DFC (9 victories) is on the left. Jones came from Altrincham, born 29 January 1893)

Captain Frank Ormond Soden
DFC*
Born Petit Codiac, New Brunswick 3 November 1895*. Died London, 12 February 1964.
8th South Staffordshire Rgt; 60 & 41 Squadrons
27 victories
(* Although born in Canada, he was British)

Captain Arthur Treloar Whealy
DSC* DFC
Born Toronto, 2 November 1893. Died St Marguerite, Quebec, 23 December 1945
3 Wing, 3 & 9 Sqns RNAS, 203 Sqn RAF
27 victories
(In the picture Art Whealy sits in the cockpit of a Camel, with Ray Collishaw. Another picture of him can be found under Hayne – 15 victories)

Captain William Frederick James Harvey
DFC*
Born Portslade, Sussex, 8 January 1897. Died Wingham, Kent, 21 July 1972
Royal Engineers (TA); 22 Squadron
26 victories

Captain Elwyn Roy King
DSO DFC
Born Bathurst, New South Wales, 13 May 1894. Died Point Cook, 28 November 1941
Australian Light Horse; 4 Squadron AFC
26 victories

Captain Gerald Joseph Constable Maxwell
MC DFC AFC
Born Inverness, 8 September 1895. Died Hampshire, 18 December 1959.
Lovat Scouts; 56 Squadron
26 victories

Captain William Ernest Staton
MC DFC* (DSO WW2)
Born 27 August 1898. Died Emsworth, Hampshire, 22 July 1983
62 Squadron
26 victories

Captain William McKenzie Thomson
MC DFC
Born Lachine Province, Quebec, 15 September 1898. Died 9 July 1987
20 Squadron
26 victories

Major Keith Logan Caldwell
MC DFC* CdG(B)
Born Wellington, New Zealand, 16 October 1895. Died 28 November 1980
NZ Territorial Infantry; 8, 60 & 74 Squadrons
25 victories

Captain Robert John Orton Compston
DSC** DFC
Born 9 January 1898. Died 28 January 1962
8 Sqn RNAS, 40 Sqn RAF
25 victories

Captain Arthur Percival Foley Rhys Davids
DSO MC*
Born Forest Hill, SE London, 26 September 1897. KIA France, 27 October 1917
56 Squadron
25 victories

Captain Stanley Wallace Rosevear
DSC*
Born Walkerton, Ontario, 9 March 1896. KIFA France, 25 April 1918
1 Sqn RNAS, 201 Sqn RAF
25 victories

Captain William Charles Campbell
DSO MC*
Born Bordeaux, France, 27 April 1889. Died Hove, 26 February 1958
1 Squadron
24 victories
(Campbell is on the right, with Philip Fullard DSO MC (40 victories) on the left)

Captain Peter Carpenter
DSO MC*
Born Cardiff, 6 December 1892.
45 & 66 Squadrons
24 victories

Captain Henry George Ernest Luchford
MC*
Born Bromley, Kent, 28 October 1894. KIA France, 2 December 1917
Army Service Corps; 20 Squadron
24 victories

Captain William Ernest Shields
DFC*
Born Lipton, Saskatchewen, 15 October 1892. KIFA Canada, 1920s
41 Squadron
24 victories
(The aeroplane is an SE5a)

Captain James Anderson Slater
MC* DFC
Born Worthing, Sussex, 27 November 1896. KIFA Upavon, 26 November 1925
Irish Rifles; 18, 1 & 64 Squadrons
24 victories

Captain Matthew Brown Frew
DSO MC* Italian Silver Medal for Military Valour
Born Glasgow, 7 April 1895. Died Pretoria, South Africa, 28 May 1974
Highland Light Infantry; 45 Squadron
23 victories

Captain Horace Percy Lale
DFC
Born Sherwood, Notts, 8 April 1896. Died 1950s
48, 39HD & 20 Squadrons
23 victories
(Lale is in the centre, flanked by Lts Kirby and Saker)

Captain Augustus Alexander Norman Dudley Pentland
MC DFC
Born Queensland, Australia, 5 August 1894. Died Bayview, NSW, 3 November 1983
12th Australian Light Horse; 19 & 87 Squadrons
23 victories

Captain Harold Alfred Whistler
DSO DFC*
Born Theddlethorpe, Lincs, 30 December 1896. KIFA Persian Gulf, 1 March 1940
Dorsetshire Rgt; 3 & 80 Squadrons
23 victories

Captain William Melville Alexander
DSC
Born Toronto, Canada, 8 November 1897. Died 4 October 1988
10 Sqn RNAS, 210 Sqn RAF
22 victories

Captain Thomas Sinclair Harrison
DFC* CdG(B)
From King William Town, South Africa, born 8 January 1898.
South African Artillery; 29 Squadron
22 victories

Captain Louis Fleeming Jenkin
MC*
Born Kensington, London, 22 August 1895. KIA France, 11 September 1917.
9th Loyal North Lancashire Rgt; 1 Squadron
22 victories

Captain Cecil Frederick King
MC DFC CdG(F)
Born Sevenoaks, Kent, 19 February 1899. KIFA 24 January 1919
Essex Rgt; 43 Squadron
22 victories

Captain John Leacroft
MC*
Born Derby, 4 November 1888. Died Bexhill, Sussex, 26 August 1971
Army Service Corps; 14 & 19 Squadrons
22 victories

Captain Benjamin Roxburgh-Smith
DFC* CdG(B)
Born Lee, SE London, 10 April 1884
65 & 74 Squadrons
22 victories

Captain Joseph Leonard Maries White
DFC* CdG
Born Halifax, Nova Scotia, 6 January 1897. KIFA 24 February 1925
Canadian Machine Gun Corps; 65 Squadron
22 victories

Major William John Charles Kennedy Cochran-Patrick
DSO MC*
Born in Edinburgh, 25 May 1896. KIFA Johannesburg, SA, 27 September 1933
Rifle Brigade; 70, 23 & 60 Squadrons
21 victories

Captain Charles Robert Reeves Hickey
DSO DFC*
From Parksville, British Columbia, born 10 September 1897. KIFA Belgium, 3 October 1918
Canadian Mounted Rifles; 4 Sqn RNAS, 204 Sqn RAF
21 victories

Captain Richard Aveline Maybery
MC*
Born Brecon, S Wales, 4 January 1895. KIA France, 19 December 1917
21st Lancers; 56 Squadron
21 victories

Captain Edgar James Kingston McCloughry
DSO DFC*
From Adelaide, born 10 September 1896. Died 15 November 1972
Australian Engineers; 23 Sqn RFC, 4 Sqn AFC
21 victories

Lieutenant Richard Pearman Minifie
DSC**
Born Melbourne, Australia, 2 February 1898. Died Melbourne, 31 March 1969
1 Wing & 1 Sqn RNAS
21 victories

Captain George Edwin Thomson
DSO MC
From Helensburgh, Dumbarton, born 19 September 1897.
KIFA Port Meadow, Oxford, 23 May 1918
King's Own Scottish Borderers; 46 Squadron
21 victories

Lieutenant Leonard Monteagle Barlow
MC**
Born Islington, London, 5 June 1898. KIFA Martlesham Heath, 5 February 1918
56 Squadron
20 victories

Captain Douglas John Bell
MC*
Born Bloemfontein, SA, 16 September 1893. KIA France, 27 May 1918
27, 78HD & 3 Squadrons
20 victories

Lieutenant Kenneth Burns Conn
DFC
Born Ashton, Ontario, 11 July 1896. Died Toronto, 30 January 1984
3rd Res Battn & 234th Battn., CEF; 88 Squadron
20 victories

Captain Edgar Charles Johnston
DFC
Born Perth, Western Australia, 30 April 1896. Died Melbourne, 22 May 1988
Australian Imperial Forces; 24 & 88 Squadrons
20 victories

Captain Camille Henri Raoul Lagesse
DFC* Cdg(B)
Born Quatre Borneo, Mauritius, 10 January 1893
29 Squadron
20 victories

Captain Ian Donald Roy McDonald
MC DFC
Born St John's, Antigua, BWI, 9 September 1898.
KOAS Dangatora, Mesopotamia, September 1921
39HD & 24 Squadrons
20 victories

Major Keith Rodney Park
MC* DFC CdG(F)
Born Thames, Auckland, NZ, 15 June 1892. Died Auckland, 6 February 1975
NZ Field Artillery; 48 Squadron
20 victories

Captain Charles Gordon Ross
DFC* CdG(B)
Born Johannesburg, South Africa, 12 March 1892. Died Durban, SA, 24 February 1969
29 Squadron
20 victories

Captain Walter Alfred Southey
DFC*
Born Bermondsey, SE London, 29 April 1897. Accidentally killed 17 April 1920
19th Royal Fusiliers; 48 & 84 Squadrons
20 victories

Captain Frederick James Harry Thayre
MC*
From London, born 20 October 1893. KIA France, 9 June 1917
Honourable Artillery Coy (Infantry); 16 & 20 Squadrons
20 victories

Captain Horace Dale Barton
DFC*
South African, born 22 November 1891
South African Army; 24 Squadron
19 victories
(Barton is on the left)

Captain Wilfred Beaver
MC
Born Kingswood, Bristol, 10 May 1897. Died West Point, Mississippi, 19 August 1986
20 Squadron
19 victories
(Became an American citizen post World War I)

Captain Andrew King Cowper
MC**
Born Bingara, NSW, Australia, 16 November 1898. Died Randwick, NSW, 25 June 1980
Royal Sussex Regt; 24 Squadron
19 victories

Captain Arthur Bradfield Fairclough
MC
Born Toronto, Canada, 25 July 1896. Died 9 December 1968
166th Rgt (MGC) CEF; 19 & 23 Squadrons
19 victories

Captain Cedric Ernest Howell
DSO MC DFC
Born Adelaide, 17 June 1896. KIFA off Corfu, Greece, 10 December 1919
46th & 14th Battns. ANZAC; 45 Squadron
19 victories
(Earl McN Hand DFC (5) sits in the doorway with Howell across his knees)

Captain Arthur Eden Reed
DFC*
From Pretoria, South Africa, born 22 August 1898.
South African Army; 29 Squadron
19 victories

Flight Sub-lieutenant Ellis Vair Reid
DSC
Born Belleville, Ontario, 31 October 1889. KIA France, 28 July 1917
3 Wing & 10 Sqn RNAS
19 victories

Lieutenant-Colonel Alan Machin Wilkinson
DSO*
Born Eastbourne, Sussex, 21 November 1891.
Hampshire Rgt TF; 24, 48 & 23 Squadrons
19 victories

Captain James Dacres Belgrave
MC
Born Kensington, London, 27 September 1896. KIA France, 13 June 1918
Oxford & Bucks Light Infantry; 45, 61HD & 60 Squadrons
18 victories

Captain George Chisholme MacKay
DFC, LdH(F), Order of Leopold(B), CdG(F)
Born Sunderland, Ontario, 17 May 1898. Died Mimico, Ont, 14 September 1973
13 Sqn RNAS, 213 Sqn RAF
18 victories

Major William Earle Molesworth
MC* Italian Bronze Medal
Irish, born in the Andaman Islands, Bay of Bengal, 14 March 1894
Royal Munster Rgt; 60 & 29 Squadrons
18 victories

Captain Maurice Ashdown Newnham
DFC* CdG(F)
From Barnes, Middx, and Woodbury, Devon, born 31 August 1897. Died October 1974
Army; 4 & 65 Squadrons
18 victories

Captain John Todd
MC DFC
Born Falkirk, Scotland, 12 January 1899
70 Squadron
18 victories

Captain John Lightfoot Trollope
MC*
Born Wallington, Surrey, 30 May 1897
Army; 70 & 43 Squadrons
18 Victories

Captain Walter Alexander Tyrell
MC
From Bangor, County Down, born 23 August 1898. KIA France, 9 June 1918
RNAS Armoured Cars; 32 Squadron
18 victories
(Tyrell is seated in an SE5a)

Captain Ronald Burns Bannerman
DFC*
Born Invercargill, NZ, 21 September 1898. Died Gore, Southland, NZ, 2 August 1978
79 Squadron
17 victories

Major Alfred William Carter
DSC MBE
Born Fish Creek, Calgary, Alberta, 29 April 1894. Died Vancouver, 17 December 1986
3 Wing, 3 & 10 Sqns RNAS, 210 Sqn RAF
17 victories

Captain Stearne Tighe Edwards
DSC*
From Carleton Place, Canada, born 13 February 1893. DoI (flying accident) 22 November 1918
2 & 3 Wings RNAS, 11, 6 & 9 Sqns RNAS, 209 Sqn RAF
17 victories

Captain Carl Frederick Falkenberg
DFC*
From Newfoundland, Canada, born 4 February 1897. Died Edmonton, 7 October 1980
Quebec Rgt; 84 Squadron
17 victories

Captain George Everard Gibbons
MC DFC
Born Stourbridge, Staffordshire, 15 February 1895.
North Staffordshire Rgt; 8, 20 & 62 Squadrons
17 victories
(Gibbons is on the right, with his observer, S.A.W. Knights on the left)

Major Fred Parkinson Holliday
DSO MC
Born Melbourne, Australia, 20 February 1888. Died in Canada, 5 March 1980
Canadian Engineers; 48 Squadron
17 victories

Lieutenant Edward Grahame Johnstone
DSC
Born London, 6 May 1899
8 Sqn RNAS, 208 Sqn RAF
17 victories

Captain John William Pinder
DFC*
Born Deal, Kent, 14 February 1898
9 & 13 Sqns RNAS, 213 & 45 Squadrons RAF
17 victories
(Pinder is in the centre, in the raincoat. The others are Taylor, W.E. Gray DFC (5), Harstmann, (Pinder) A.R. Talbot and Hancock)

Captain Edwin Swale
DFC*
Born Chesterfield, 28 June 1899. Died August 1978
10 Sqn RNAS, 210 Squadron RAF
17 victories

Captain Edmund Roger Tempest
MC DFC
Born Pontefract, Yorkshire, 30 October 1894
King's Own Yorkshire Light Infantry; 6, 29, 15 & 64 Squadrons
17 victories

Captain Own Morgan Baldwin
DFC* LdH(F) CdG(F)
Born Twyford, Berkshire, 21 February 1893. Died Berkshire, 12 January 1942
73 Squadron
16 victories

Captain Gerald Gordon Bell
DFC LdH(F)
Born Ottawa, 11 June 1890
38th Battn. East Ontario Rgt, CEF; 22, 17, 47 & 150 Squadrons
16 victories

Captain Henry John Burden
DSO DFC
Born Canada, 28 April 1893. Died Toronto, 28 March 1960
11th Machine Gun Company; 56 Squadron
16 victories

Captain John Stanley Chick
MC
From Pontardawe, Wales, born 22 September 1897. Died Colchester, 21 January 1960
11 Squadron
16 victories

Sergeant Ernest John Elton
DCM MM Italian Bronze Medal
Born Wimborne, Dorset, 25 December 1893. Died Taplow Bucks, 8 March 1958
22 Squadron
16 victories

Captain Robert Mordaunt Foster
DFC
Born 3 September 1898. Died 23 October 1973
Royal Fusiliers; 54 & 209 Squadrons
16 victories

Captain George Brian Gates
DFC*
Born Hove, Sussex, 21 July 1899
1 Sqn RNAS, 201 Sqn RAF
16 victories

Captain The Honorable Robert Arthur Grosvenor
MC*
Born Chester, 25 May 1895. Died Chaddleworth, Berks, 12 June 1953
2nd Dragoon Guards; 57 & 84 Squadrons
16 victories

Captain Allan Hepburn
DFC
Born Melbourne Australia, 11 October 1896. Died 21 July 1975
Artists' Rifles; 24, 40 & 88 Squadrons
16 victories

Captain Sidney William Highwood
DFC*
From Marden, Kent, born 30 December 1896
84 Squadron
16 victories

Sergeant Frank Johnson
DCM*
Born Oldham, Lancashire, 26 December 1896
22 (Obs), 20 & 62 Squadrons
16 victories
(Four victories as an observer, 12 as a pilot)

Captain Oliver William Redgate
DFC
Born Nottingham, 23 November 1894
9 Sqn RNAS, 209 Sqn RAF
16 victories

Captain Francis Ryan Smith
MC DFC
Born Brisbane, Australia, 1896
Australian infantry; 2 Sqn AFC
16 victories

Captain Christoffel Johannes Venter
DFC*
Born Middelburg, Cape, SA, 1 November 1893. Died SA, 20 February 1977
29 Squadron
16 victories

Captain Lawrence Percival Coombes
DFC
Born in India, 9 April 1899. Died Melbourne, 2 June 1988
10 Sqn RNAS, 210 Sqn RAF
15 victories

Major Cyril Marconi Crowe
MC DFC
Born County Durham, 6 January 1894. Died in 1974
4, 8, 16, 56, 60 & 85 Squadrons
15 victories

Captain Charles William Cudemore
MC DFC
From Essex, born 19 November 1897
King's Scottish Light Infantry; 40, 29 & 64 Squadrons
15 victories
(Cudemore is on the right; A.G. Jones-Williams MC (11) on the left)

Lieutenant Ralph Luxmore Curtis
Born Braintree, Essex, 19 March 1896. DoW, Belgium, 21 September 1917
48 Squadron
15 victories

Captain James Fitz-Morris+
MC*
Born Falkirk, Scotland, 6 April 1897. KIFA Indianapolis, USA, 14 August 1918
11, 25 & 23 Squadrons
15 victories
(+ also recorded as J.F. Morris, Fitzmorris and Fitzmaurice)

Captain James Alpheus Glen
DSC* CdG(F)
From Turtle Mountain, Manitoba, Canada, born 23 June 1890. Died England, 7 March 1962
3 Sqn RNAS, 203 Sqn RAF
15 victories
(centre with the camera)

Lieutenant Harry King Goode
DSO DFC
Born Handsworth, nr Birmingham, 22 October 1992. KOAS 21 August 1942
Royal Engineers; 66 Squadron
15 victories

Captain John Edmund Greene
DFC
Born Winnipeg, Canada, 2 July 1894. KIA Belgium, 14 October 1918
13 Sqn RNAS, 213 Sqn RAF
15 victories
(Greene is on the left, with L.H. Slatter DSC DFC (7) on the right)

Captain Edwin Tufnell Hayne
DSC DFC
From South Africa, born 28 May 1895. KIFA Castle Bromwich, 28 April 1919
3 Sqn RNAS, 203 Sqn RAF
15 victories
(Hayne is on the left, with Art Whealy DSC DFC (27) and H.F. Beamish DSC (11))

Captain Andrew Cameron Kiddie
DFC* CdG(B)
Born Kimberley, SA, 7 November 1889. Died Kimberley, June 1964
South African Army; 74 Squadron
15 victories

Captain Harold Thomas Mellings
DSC* DFC, Greek Silver War Medal
Born in Ludlow, Shropshire, 5 August 1897. KIA France, 25 July 1918
2 Wing & 10 Sqn RNAS, 210 Sqn RAF
15 victories

Major Roy Cecil Phillipps
MC* DFC
Born Sydney, Australia, 1 March 1892. KIFA (Buried Brisbane) 21 May 1940
28th Infantry Battn. AIF; 32 Sqn RFC, 2 Sqn AFC
15 victories

Captain Hugh William Lumsden Saunders
MC DFC MM
From Transvaal, South Africa, born 24 August 1894. Died 8 May 1987
South African Horse; 84 Squadron
15 victories

Captain Harold Francis Stackard
From Muswell Hill, born Norwich, Norfolk, 2 March, 1895
RN Division; 9 Sqn RNAS
15 victories

Captain Frank Gerald Craven Weare
MC
Born Ferndale, Tunbridge Wells, Kent. Died Sussex, 6 July 1971
2nd Battn, The Queens; 22 Squadron
15 victories

Captain Colin Peter Brown
DFC*
From Sydenham, born 20 December 1898. Died 19 October 1965
13 Sqn RNAS, 213 Sqn RAF
14 victories

Captain Carleton Main Clement
MC CdG
From Canada, born 15 May 1896. KIA France, 19 August 1917
47th Battn. CEF; 22 Squadron
14 victories

Major Arthur Coningham
DSO MC
Born Brisbane, Australia, 19 January 1895. KIFA off Bermuda, 30 January 1948
NZ Canterbury Mounted Rifles; 32 & 92 Squadrons
14 victories

Captain Charles Findlay
DFC
From Scotland, born 22 June 1891
6th Battn. Highland Light Infantry; 88 Squadron
14 victories

Captain Maxwell Hutcheon Findlay
DSC DFC
Born Aberdeen, Scotland, 17 February 1898. KIFA N. Rhodesia, October 1936
Black Watch; 6 & 1 Sqns RNAS, 201 Sqn RAF
14 victories

Captain Frank George Gibbons
DFC
Born Peterborough, 13 June 1899. KIFA Stanton, Norfolk, 21 May 1932
Northumberland Rgt; 22 Squadron
14 victories

Captain Albert Earl Godfrey
MC
From Vancouver, Canada, born 27 July 1890. Died Kingston, Ontario, 1 January 1982
10, 25, 40, 44HD & 78HD Squadrons
14 victories

Captain Frank Clifford Gorringe
MC DFC
From Eastbourne, Sussex, born 30 September 1889
43 (Obs), 70 and 210 Squadrons
14 victories

Major Arthur Willan Keen
MC
Born Birmingham, 20 March 1895. DoI (Flying accident) France, 12 September 1918
Army Service Corps; 70 & 40 Squadrons
14 victories

Captain Maurice Edmund Mealing
MC
Born High Wycombe, Bucks, 21 July 1893. KIA France, 24 March 1918
King's Shropshire Light Infantry; 15 & 56 Squadron
14 victories

Captain James Dennis Payne
MC
From Leamington Spa, born 22 July 1887
41 & 29 Squadrons
14 victories

Lieutenant William Sidebottom
DFC
Born Manchester, 11 October 1893
203 Squadron
14 victories

Captain Jack Victor Sorsoleil
MC
Born Toronto, Canada, 2 June 1898. DOAS RCAF, 1946
84 Squadron
14 victories

Captain Arthur Whitehair Vigers
MC DFC
Born Denmark Hill, London, 20 January 1890. Died Australia, September 1968
Royal Engineers; 15 & 87 Squadrons
14 victories

Captain Hazel LeRoy Wallace
DFC
Born Lethbridge, Alberta, 13 November 1897. Died 22 March 1976
9 Sqn RNAS, 201 & 3 Sqns RAF
14 victories

Captain Herbert Gillies Watson
DFC
Born Caversham, Dunedin, New Zealand, 30 March 1889. Died 1940s
Australian Army Service Corps; 4 Sqn AFC
14 victories
(Watson is on the left, E.J.K. McCloughry DFC to the right)

Captain Noel William Ward Webb
MC*
Born Margate, Kent, 12 December 1896. KIA France, 16 August 1917
25 & 70 Squadrons
14 victories

Captain Thomas Frederic Williams
MC Italian Silver Medal
Born Ontario, Canada, 12 October 1885. Died Woodstock, Ontario, July 1985
1st Canadian Div; 45 & 28 Squadrons
14 victories

Captain Reginald Milburn Makepeace (NO PHOTO)
MC
Born Liverpool, 27 December 1887. KIFA Turnberry, 28 May 1918
20 & 11 Squadrons
17 victories

Captain Frank Hobson (NO PHOTO)
MC
From West Bridgford, Nottingham, born 8 October 1894
Royal Engineers; 70 Squadron
15 victories

Lieutenant Herbert Brian Richardson (NO PHOTO)
MC DFC
From Ashford, Kent, born 27 May 1898.
KIFA Cuatro Vientos, nr Madrid, Spain, 14 February 1922
Oxford & Bucks Light Infantry; 24 Squadron
15 victories

Captain Ronald Turnbull Mark (NO PHOTO)
MC*
From Newcastle-on-Tyne, born 1898
24 Squadron
14 victories

Flight Commander Frederick Carr Armstrong
DSC CdG
Born Toronto, 19 June 1895. KIA, France, 25 March 1918
3 Sqn RNAS
13 victories

Captain Charles Chaplin Banks
MC DFC
From Llandulus, Denbighshire
5th Battn. Royal Welsh Fusiliers; 44HD & 43 Squadrons
13 victories
(Banks is sitting in Sopwith Snipe)

Captain Reginald Carey Brenton Brading
DFC*
Born Addiscombe, Surrey, 4 May 1899. KIFA Hinaidi, Iraq, 26 July 1926
1 Sqn RNAS, 201 Sqn RAF
13 victories
(In this picture Brading is second from the right. Others from the left are, W.E.G. Mann DFC (13), A. Coningham DSO MC DFC (14), T.F.N. Gerrard DSC (10), and C. Draper DSC (9) far right: Hendon Air Pageant 1921)

Captain Geoffrey Hornblower Cock
MC
Born Shrewsbury, Salop, 7 January 1896. Died 16 February 1980
28th London Rgt; 45 Squadron
13 victories

Captain Douglas Graham Cooke
MC
Born London, 26 July 1895
20 Squadron
13 victories
(Cooke is on the right, with his observer H.G. Crowe MC)

Captain Jack Cottle
DFC Italian Silver Medal
Born Plymouth, S Devon, 19 June 1892. Died India, 15 August 1967
South African Mounted Rifles; 45 Squadron
13 victories

Captain Wilfred Austin Curtis
DSC*
Born Havelock, Ontario, born 21 August 1893. Died 7 August 1977
6 & 10 Sqns RNAS
13 victories

Captain Albert James Enstone
DSC DFC
From Birmingham, born 29 August 1895
4 Sqn RNAS, 204 Sqn RAF
13 victories

Lieutenant Gavin Lynedoch Graham
DFC LdH(F) CdG
Born 18 October 1894, Grahamstown, South Africa
18th Hussars; 70, 73 & 78HD Squadrons
13 victories
(Graham is on the left, with E.J. Lussier DFC (11))

Captain Harold Alan Hamersley
MC
Born Guildford, Western Australia, 6 February 1896. Died December 1967
Australian Army; 60 Squadron
13 victories
(Hamersley is on the far right, with E. Thornton, R.L. Chidlaw-Roberts MC (10) and J.B. Crompton (5))

Captain Oscar Aloysius Patrick Heron
DFC CdG(B)
Born Armagh City, Ireland, 17 September 1896
Connaught Rangers; 70 Squadron
13 victories

Captain Spencer Bertram Horn
MC
Born Rebrass, Salisbury, England, 18 April 1895
Dragoon Guards; 60 & 85 Squadrons
13 victories

Captain George Robert Howsam
MC
From Toronto, Canada, born 21 January 1895. Died Victoria, BC, 16 April 1988
70 & 43 Squadrons
13 victories

Lieutenant Ernest Charles Hoy
DFC
Born Dauphin, Manitoba, Canada, 6 May 1895. Died Toccoa, Georgia, USA, 11 April 1982
29 Squadron
13 victories

Lieutenant Harold Byron Hudson
MC
Born Cobham, Surrey, England, 8 December 1898. Died Vancouver, BC, February 1982
28 & 45 Squadrons
13 victories

Captain Soloman Clifford Joseph
DFC*
Born Edgbaston, Birmingham, England, 29 April 1893
10 Sqn RNAS, 210 Sqn RAF
13 victories

Captain Ronald McNeill Keirstead
DSC
From Wolfville, Nova Scotia, born 20 June 1895. Died Wolfville, 23 October 1970
4 Sqn RNAS, 204 Sqn RAF
13 victories

Captain John Herbert Towne Letts
MC
From Lincoln, born 10 June 1897. KIFA France, 11 October 1918
27, 48, 64 & 87 Squadrons
13 victories

Captain William Edward George Mann
DFC
Born 20 April 1899. Died 4 May 1966
208 Squadron
13 victories
(Mann is on the far right, with J.B. White DFC (12) and C. Draper DSC (9))

Captain John Gerald Manuel
DSC
Born Edmonton, Alberta, 29 March 1893. KIFA France, 10 June 1918
Canadian Field Artillery; 10 Sqn RNAS, 210 Sqn RAF
13 victories

Captain Wilfred Reid May
DFC
Born Edmonton, Canada, 20 March 1896. Died 21 June 1952
202nd Battn. Canadian Infantry; 209 Squadron
13 victories

Captain Thomas Laurence Purdom
MC
Born Hawick, Scotland, 24 June 1892
4/King's Own Scottish Borderers; 15 & 62 Squadrons
13 victories
(Purdom is on the left, his observer P.V. Chambers on the right)

Captain Harry Gosford Reeves
Born Staines Middlesex, 30 September 1897. KIFA France, 24 January 1918
Artist's Rifles; 1 Squadron
13 victories
(In this group, Reeves stands second from the left, arm in arm with Philip Fullard DSO MC (40). W.W. Rogers MC (9) is 4th from the right. C.S.I. Lavers DFC (9) is 3rd from left astride the shoulders of F.M. Maclaren)

Lieutenant George Raby Riley
MC DFC
From Clapham, SW London, born 23 February 1899
3 Squadron
13 victories

Major Frederick Sowrey
DSO MC
Born Twigworth, Glos., 25 August 1893. Died Eastbourne, Sussex, 21 Oct 1968
39HD, 37HD, 19 and 143 HD Squadrons
13 victories

Captain Stanley Stanger
MC DFC
Born Montreal, Canada, 10 July 1894. Died Montreal, 10 September 1967
1st Canadian Artillery; 66 & 28 Squadrons
13 victories

Captain Eric John Stephens
DFC
From Western Australia, 13 September 1895.
41 Squadron
13 victories
(The picture shows Stephens in front of his SE5, holding a 25 lb bomb)

Captain Francis Stanley Symondson
MC Italian Silver Medal
Born Sutton, Surrey, 27 March 1897. Died Lyme Regis, 1 May 1975
Glamorgan Yeomanry; 29 & 66 Squadrons
13 victories

Captain Oliver Henry Douglas Vickers
From Mayfair, London W1, born 12 September 1898
20 Squadron
13 victories

Lieutenant Walter Bertram Wood
MC*
Born Grimsby, Lincolnshire, 25 October 1898. KOAS Hainault Farm, 11 November 1917
Hampshire Rgt; 29 & 44HD Squadrons
13 victories

Major John Oliver Andrews
DSO MC*
Born Waterloo, Lancashire, 20 July 1896. Died 29 May 1989
Royal Scottish Rgt; 5, 24, 66 & 209 Squadrons
12 victories

Major Brian Edmund Baker
DSO MC
Born Hertford, 31 August 1896. Died Fife, Scotland, 8 October 1979
Rifle Brigade; 48 & 141HD Squadrons
12 victories

Captain Thomas Charles Richmond Baker
DFC MM*
Born Smithfield, South Australia, 2 May 1897. KIA France, 4 November 1918
6th Field Artillery Bde; 4 Sqn AFC
12 victories

Lieutenant Gerald Alfred Birks
MC*
From Montreal, Canada, born 30 October 1894. Died Toronto, 26 May 1991
66 Squadron
12 victories

Major Christopher Joseph Quintin Brand
DSO MC DFC
From Kimberley, South Africa, born 25 May 1893. Died Rhodesia, 9 March 1968
1, 112 & 151 Squadrons
12 victories

Captain Raymond James Brownell
MC MM
Born Tasmania, 17 May 1894. Died Perth, Western Australia, 12 April 1974
Australian Artillery; 45 Squadron
12 victories

Captain Oliver Campbell Bryson
MC
From Worcestershire, born 18 August 1896. Died 27 March 1977
Queen's Own Dorset Yeomanry Cavalry; 19 Squadron
12 victories
(Bryson is standing 3rd from the left; seated: J.G.S. Candy DFC (6), E. Olivier (8), Reid-Walker; standing: H.V. Puckridge DFC, J. Leacroft MC* (22), Bryson, P. Huskinson MC* (11))

Captain Walter Macfarlane Carlaw
DFC
Born Glasgow, 8 March 1899
70 Squadron
12 victories

Lieutenant Edward Arnold Clear
MC
From London, born Islington, 28 May 1896
84 Squadron
12 victories
(In this picture Clear is sitting bare-headed in the front. Standing l to r: Graeme Leask MC (8), F.E. Brown MC (10), G.O. Johnson MC (11) and Northcote. Sitting: A.F. W.B. Proctor VC DSO MC DFC (54), Clear, Payne? and W E Lunnon)

Captain Francis James Davies
DFC
From Warwickshire, born 20 October 1889
29 Squadron
12 victories

Captain William Leeming Harrison
MC
From Toronto, born 1898. Died in Canada, 1960s
Canterbury Mounted Rifles; 40 & 1 Squadrons
12 victories

Captain William Henry Hubbard
DFC*
Born Kingston, Ontario, 19 May 1886. Died Canada, 19 June 1960
7, 5 & 73 Squadrons
12 victories

Captain John Ellis Langford Hunter
DSC DFC
Born Tynemouth, Northumberland, 31 January 1897
4 Sqn RNAS, 204 Sqn RAF
12 victories
(Hunter is on the right with W. Sidebottom DFC (14) and Nick Carter(17))

Captain George Budd Irving
DFC
Born Toronto, Canada, 16 May 1898. KIA France, 11 August 1918
19 Squadron
12 victories

Captain William Stanley Jenkins
DFC*
Born Montreal, Canada, 26 May 1890
87th Battn. Canadian Infantry; 210 Squadron
12 victories
(Bottom left is E. Swale DFC (17))

Captain Gwilym Hugh Lewis
DFC
Born Mosely, Birmingham, 5 August 1897. Died London, 17 December 1996
2/4 Northampton Rgt; 32 & 40 Squadrons
12 victories

Captain Roby Lewis Manuel
DFC
Born Kerang, Victoria, 7 October 1895. Died 18 October 1975
Australian Infantry; 2 Sqn AFC
12 victories

Lieutenant Norman William Reginald Mawle
DFC
Born Banbury, Oxon, 27 February 1897. Died Leicester, 28 December 1971
London Regiment; 7 & 84 Squadrons
12 victories
(Mawle is on the left, with C.R. Thompson DFC (6))

Captain Douglas Urchart McGregor
MC
Born Waterdown, Ontario, Canada, March 1895. Died in 1953
23 Squadron
12 victories

Captain Kenneth Barbour Montgomery
MC Italian Croce di Guerra
From Oxton, Cheshire, born 22 October 1897
45 & 66 Squadrons
12 victories

Captain Ian Patrick Robert Napier
MC LdH(F) CdG(F)
From Bowling, Dumbartonshire, born 24 July 1895. Died London, 9 May 1977
Argyll & Sutherland Highlanders; 40 Squadron
12 victories

Flight Commander Guy William Price
DSC*
From Dublin, Eire, born 6 July 1895. KIA France, 18 February 1918
13 & 8 Sqns RNAS
12 victories

Captain John Steele Ralston
DFC
Born Edinburgh, 27 April 1887. KIA France, 25 July 1918
71, 84 & 24 Squadrons
12 victories

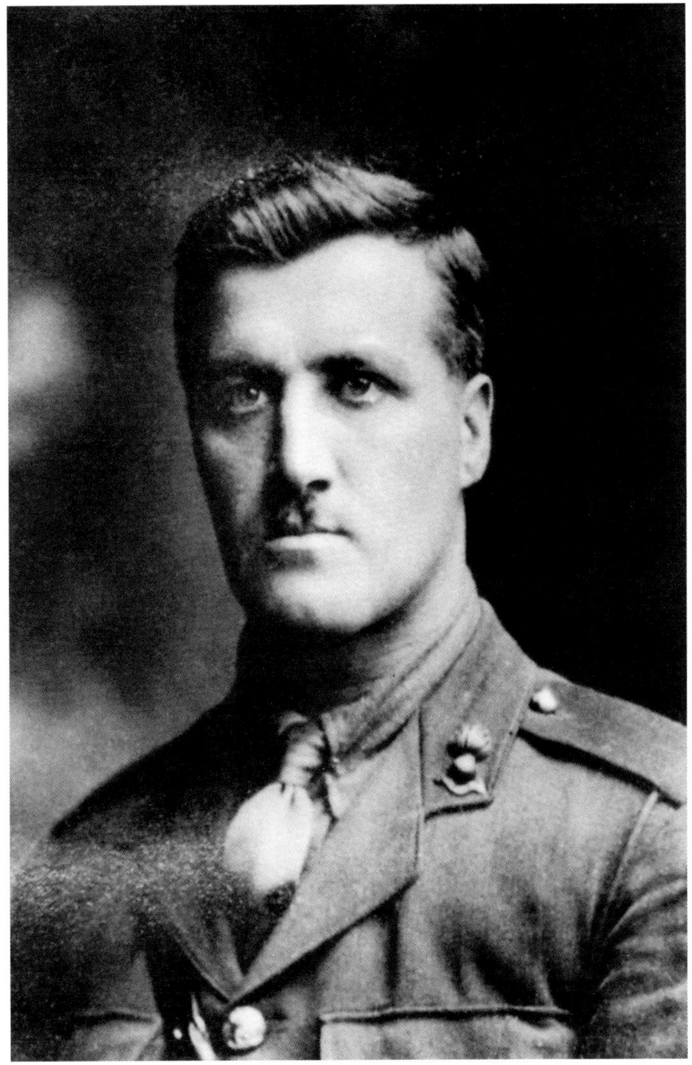

Captain Alfred William Saunders
DFC
Born Dublin, Eire, 16 January 1888
Royal Field Artillery; 60 Squadron
12 victories

Captain Maurice Douglas Guest Scott
MC
From Felixstowe, born 13 August 1895. KIFA Shoreham, 17 March 1918
3rd Loyal North Lancashire Rgt; 18, 54 & 46 Squadrons
12 victories
(Scott is on the left, with C.W. Odell (6))

Major Alexander MacDonald Shook
DSO DSC CdG
Born Tioga, Ontario, 2 December 1888. Died Bala, Ontario, 30 May 1966
5 Wing & 4 Sqn RNAS, 204 Sqn RAF
12 victories

Captain Reginald Rhys Soar
DSC
Born Castleford, Yorks, 24 August 1893. Died Martletwy, Pembroke, in 1971
3 & 5 Wings, 8 Sqn RNAS
12 victories
(Soar is on the right, with B.L. Huskisson DSC)

Captain William Samuel Stephenson
MC DFC
Born Winnipeg, Canada, 11 January 1896. Died Bermuda, January 1989
Canadian Engineers; 73 Squadron
12 victories

Lieutenant Leonard Thomas Eaton Taplin
DFC
Born Adelaide, Australia, 16 December 1895. Died Perth, 8 July 1961
Australian Engineers; 67 Sqn RFC, 1 & 4 Sqns AFC
12 victories

Lieutenant Chester William McKinley Thompson
British subject, born N Woburn, Massachusetts, USA, 11 April 1899. Lies buried in Dartford, Kent.
22 Squadron
12 victories
(In this group, Thompson is second from the right. Extreme right is G.W. Bulmer MC (9). From l to r: P. Stayle (Obs), I.O. Stead (P)(5), H.J. Weaver (Obs), H.H. Beddow (P)(10), W.F.J. Harvey DFC (P)(26), J.E. Gurdon DFC (P)(28), G. Thomson (Obs) C.W.M. Thompson and Bulmer)

Captain Adrian James Boswell Tonks
DFC*
From Kensington, London, born 10 May 1898. KIFA Egypt, 14 July 1919
4 Sqn RNAS, 204 Sqn RAF
12 victories

Captain Richard Michael Trevethan
MC
British subject born USA, 24 January 1898
20 Squadron
12 victories

Captain James Butler White
DFC
From Manitoulin Island, Ontario, born 7 July 1893. Died 2 January 1972
8 Sqn RNAS, 208 Sqn RAF
12 victories

Captain Sydney Tyndall Liversedge (NO PHOTO)
Born Huddersfield, 15 August 1897
1st Life Guards; 70 Squadron
13 victories

Lieutenant David John Weston (NO PHOTO)
DFC
Born Clapham, SW London, 14 November 1898
20 Squadron
13 victories

Captain Ernest Claude Bromley (NO PHOTO)
MC
Born Winnipeg, Canada, 18 August 1888
Canadian Engineers; 22 Squadron
12 victories

Lieutenant Henry Coyle Rath (NO PHOTO)
DFC
From Tweed, Ontario, born 12 November 1898. DoI France, 26 October 1918
29 Squadron
12 victories

Flight Commander Fred Everest Banbury
DSC
Born Regina, Saskatchewan, 27 October 1894. KIFA France, 1 April 1918
9 Sqn RNAS
11 victories
(The aeroplane is a Sopwith Camel)

Captain Harold Francis Beamish
DSC
Born Havelock North, New Zealand, 7 July 1896. Died Havelock, 26 October 1986
3 Sqn RNAS, 203 Sqn RAF
11 victories

Captain Alexander Beck
DFC
From Argentina, of Cumbrian parents, born 3 November 1898
60 Squadron
11 victories

Captain Phillip Scott Burge
MC MM
Born Potters Bar, Middx, 29 March 1895. KIA France, 24 July 1918
Army; 64 Squadron
11 victories

Flight Commander Arnold Jaques Chadwick
DSC
From Toronto, born 23 August 1895. KIA (drowned) 28 July 1917
5 Wing & 4 Sqn RNAS
11 victories

Captain Roy Williamson Chappell
MC
From South Africa, born 31 December 1896. Died late 1980s
Hartigan's Horse; 27 & 41 Squadrons
11 victories

Captain Clive Franklyn Collett
MC*
From Blenheim, New Zealand, born 28 August 1886. KIFA nr Edinburgh, 23 December 1917
70 Squadron
11 victories

Lieutenant Hiram Frank Davison
MC
Born Ontario, Canada, 12 January 1894. Died London, Ontario, January 1974
Canadian Horse Artillery; 22 Squadron
11 victories
(Davison is in the fur-lined flying suit)

Flight Lieutenant Harold Day
DSC
Born Abergavenny, Wales, 17 April 1897. KIA France, 5 February 1918
10 & 8 Sqns RNAS
11 victories

Captain William James Arthur Duncan
MC*
Born Sault Ste. Marie, Ontario, 4 July 1891. Died Aurora, Ontario, 15 April 1975
228th Battn. CEF; 60 Squadron
11 victories

Captain Trevor Durrant
Born Woking, Surrey, 21 January 1893. KIA France, 16 May 1918
55 & 56 Squadrons
11 victories

Captain John Charles Bradley Firth
MC Italian Bronze Medal
Born 8 August 1894. Died Blyth, Nottinghamshire, 23 August 1931
5th King's Somerset Light Infantry; 45 Squadron
11 victories

Captain Henry Garnet Forrest
DFC
Born Melbourne, Australia, 5 December 1895
Australian Infantry, AIF; 43, 32 & 68 Sqns RFC, 2 Sqn AFC
11 victories

Captain Williams Mays Fry
MC
Born Exmoor, Somerset, 4 November 1896. Died Blackheath, SE London, 4 August 1992
Somerset Light Infantry: 12, 11, 60, 23 & 79 Squadrons
11 victories

Captain Charles Duncan Bremner Green
DFC CdG(F)
Born Toronto, Canada, 14 August 1897.
KOAS (flying accident), nr. Toronto, Ontario, 3 October 1941
164th Battn. CEF; 47 & 150 Squadrons
11 victories

Captain Leslie Norman Hollinghurst
DFC
Born Middlesex, 2 January 1895. Died London, 8 June 1971
Royal Engineers; 3rd Battn. Middlesex Rgt; 87 Squadron
11 victories
(The aeroplane is a Sopwith Dolphin)

Captain Geoffrey Forrest Hughes
MC AFC
Born Sydney, Australia, 12 July 1895. Died 13 September 1951
62 Squadron
11 victories
(Hughes is seated in a Bristol Fighter)

Major Patrick Huskinson
MC*
From Harrow, born 17 March 1896. Died 24 November 1966
1st Battn. Sherwood Forresters; 2 & 19 Squadrons
11 victories

Captain William Roy Irwin
DFC*
From Ripley, Ontario, born 7 June 1898. Died Ottawa, 14 January 1969
56 Squadron
11 victories

Captain Mansell Richard James
DFC
From Leamington, Ontario, born 18 June 1893. KIFA (air race) 28 May 1919
45 Squadron
11 victories
(James is second from the left; from l to r: C.G. Catto (6), James, J.R. Black, F.S. Bowles (5), Doc Smith, A. Rice-Oxley DFC(6))

Captain George Owen Johnson
MC CdG(F)
Born Woodstock, Ontario, 24 January 1896. Died Florida, USA, 24 March 1980
CSCI; 84 & 24 Squadrons
11 victories

Captain Arthur Gordon Jones-Williams
MC*
Born 6 October 1898. KIFA Tunisia, 17 December 1929
Welsh Rgt; 29 & 65 Squadrons
11 victories
(J-W on left with M.A. Newnham DFC* (18)

Captain Herbert Joseph Larkin
DFC CdG(F)
Born South Brisbane, Queensland, 8 October 1894.
Died St. Martins, Channel Islands, 20 June 1972
Royal Engineers; 5 & 87 Squadrons
11 victories

Captain Walter Hunt Longton
DFC** AFC
From Lancashire, born 10 September 1892. KIFA (air race) Bournemouth, June 1927
85 & 24 Squadrons
11 victories

Captain Roy Manzer
DFC
Born Maple Creek, Saskatchewan, 31 August 1896. Died Victoria, BC, 26 August 1956
84 Squadron
11 victories

Captain Charles Midgley Maud
DFC Italian War Cross
Born Pool, West Yorkshire, 1 April 1896
Royal Artillery; 66 Squadron
11 victories

Captain Malcolm Charles McGregor
DFC*
Born nr. Hunterville, New Zealand, 4 March 1896. KIFA Wellington NZ, 19 February 1936
54 & 85 Squadrons
11 victories

Captain James Hart Mitchell
MC DFC Italian Bronze Medal
Born Hereford, 8 May 1899
Essex Rgt; 28 Squadron
11 victories

Captain Harold Anthony Oaks
DFC
Born nr. Hespelar, Ontario, 12 November 1896. Died July 1968
Canadian Engineers; 48 Squadron
11 victories
(Oaks is in the centre flanked by Maj K.R. Park MC DFC (20) and L.A. Payne MC (11))

Captain Herbert Andrew Patey
DFC
From West Hampstead, London, born 25 September 1898. Died (influenza) 18 February 1919
RN Division; 10 Sqn RNAS, 210 Sqn RAF
11 victories

Captain Leonard Allen Payne
MC
From Swaziland, South Africa, born 15 July 1894. KIFA Cologne, 18 February 1919
48 Squadron
11 victories
(see also picture H.A. Oaks (11))

Lieutenant Clement Wattson Payton
DFC
Born Ashbourne, Derbyshire, 13 April 1897. KIA Belgium, 2 October 1918
RNAS; 210 Squadron
11 victories

Captain George Ebben Randall
DFC
From London, born 19 January 1899
3 & 20 Squadrons
11 victories

Captain Cecil Roy Richards
MC
From Garvoc, Victoria, born 24 July 1893. Died Glenelg, South Australia, 19 August 1973
ANZAC; 20 Squadron
11 victories

Captain Cyril Burfield Ridley
DSC
Born Esher, Surrey, 15 January 1895. KIFA Cologne, 17 May 1920
1 Sqn RNAS, 201 Sqn RAF
11 victories

Captain Thomas Rose
DFC
Born Chilbolton, Hampshire, 27 January 1895. Died Alderney, Channel Islands, 20 June 1968
64 Squadron
11 victories

Lieutenant Ivan Couper Sanderson
DFC
From Gerrards Cross, Bucks, born 21 December 1899
210 Squadron
11 victories

Captain Ross MacPherson Smith
MC* DFC** AFC
Born Adelaide, South Australia, 4 December 1892. KIFA 14 April 1922
Australian Light Horse; 67 Sqn RAF, 1 Sqn AFC
11 victories

Lieutenant Arthur William Wood
Born Heaton, West Yorkshire, 9 April 1898
9 Sqn RNAS
11 victories

Major Wilfred Ernest Young
DFC
From Bournemouth, born 28 December 1891
Dorset Rgt; 6, 19, 74 & 1 Squadrons
11 victories
(Young is seated on the right. Seated l to r: E. Mannock VC DSO MC (73), K.L. Caldwell MC DFC (25), -?- and Young. Standing: B. Roxburgh-Smith DFC (22) and A.C. Kiddie DFC (15))

Lieutenant Edgar Oxenham Amm
DFC CdG(B)
Born Johannesburg, South Africa, 19 August 1898
29 Squadron
10 victories

Lieutenant Gordon Frank Mason Apps
DFC
Born Maidstone, Kent, 3 May 1899
66 Squadron
10 victories
(Apps is standing 5th from the left. The pilots immediately in front of him are P. Wilson MC (roll-neck sweater)(7), H.B. Hudson MC (13) and S. Stanger MC DFC (13). Another ace, J. Mackereth (7) is second from the left)

Captain Edward Dawson Atkinson
DFC AFC
A Scot, born in India 10 November 1891, and raised in Ireland
40th Pathans Rgt; 1, 56, 22 & 64 Squadrons
10 victories

Lieutenant Herbert Howell Beddow
From Cardiff, born 19 December 1898
22 Squadron
10 victories
(Beddow is standing 4th from the left. Full caption see C.W.M. Thompson (11), page 120)

Captain Hilliard Brooke Bell
MC Italian Bronze Medal
From Toronto, born 9 March 1897. Died 16 September 1960
Canadian Field Artillery; 66 Squadron
10 victories

Captain Robert Alexander Birkbeck
DFC
Born in Bournemouth, 8 October 1898
1 Squadron
10 victories

Major Lloyd Samuel Breadner
DSC
Born Carleton Place, Ontario, 17 July 1894. Died Boston, USA, 1953
3 Wing & 3 Sqn RNAS
10 victories

Captain Arthur Roy Brown
DSC*
Born Carleton Place, Ontario, 23 December 1893. Died Stouffville, Ontario, 9 March 1944
9 & 4 Sqns, RNAS, 209 Sqn RAF
10 victories

Captain Frederic Elliott Brown
MC* CdG(F)
Born Quebec, 1895. Died Toronto, 15 September 1971
Royal Dublin Fusiliers; 2 (Obs) & 84 Squadrons
10 victories

Lieutenant Patrick Anthony Byrne
DSO
From Drogheda, County Louth, Eire, born 12 November 1894. KIA France, 16 October 1916
Royal Artillery; 24 Squadron
10 victories
(also known as Langan-Byrne)

Captain Sydney Carlin
MC DFC DCM
Born Hull, 24 March 1891. KOAS RAF Wittering, 9 May 1941
Royal Engineers; 74 Squadron
10 victories

Captain Robert Leslie Chidlaw-Roberts
MC
Born May 1896. Died Winchester, 1 June 1989
2 (Obs), 18, 60 & 40 Squadrons
10 victories

Lieutenant-Colonel Jack Armand Cunningham
DSO DFC Order of Leopold(B) CdG
Born Liverpool, 4 December 1890
Royal Field Artillery; 18, 6, 65 Squadrons, 65 Wing
10 victories

Lieutenant Douglas Arthur Davies
DFC CdG(F)
Born Harrow, Middx, 12 January 1896
150 Squadron
10 victories

Lieutenant Edgar George Davies
DFC*
From Tufnell Park, London, born 4 November 1898.
KIFA Bickendorff, Germany, 6 February 1919
29 Squadron
10 victories

Captain Robert Dodds
MC
From Hamilton, Ontario, born 11 March 1892. Died Hamilton, 8 December 1990
48 Squadron
10 victories

Captain Aubrey Beauclerk Ellwood
DSC
Born Cottesmore, Rutland, 3 July 1897. Died Crewkerne, Somerset, 20 December 1992
3 Sqn RNAS
10 victories

Captain Cecil Vernon Gardner
DFC
Born Boughton, Bucks, 1891. DoW France, 30 September 1918
19 Squadron
10 victories

Major Thomas Francis Netterville Gerrard
DSC CdG
Born 30 August 1897. KOAS (F/Lt) (sport accident) 14 July 1923
'A' Sqn, 1 Sqn, RNAS, 208 and 209 Sqns RAF
10 victories

Captain Gerald Ernest Gibbs
MC** LdH(F)
Born Norwood, Surrey, 3 September 1896. Died Kingston, Surrey, 13 October 1992
8th Wiltshire Rgt; 17 & 150 Squadrons
10 victories

Major Stanley James Goble
DSO DSC
Born Croyden, Victoria, Australia, 21 August 1891. Died Melbourne, 24 July 1948
1 Wing, 8 & 5 Sqns RNAS, 205 Sqn RAF
10 victories

Lieutenant George Stacey Hodson
Born Belmont, Surrey, 2 May 1899. Died 1 October 1976
73 & 213 Squadrons
10 victories
(Hodson is in the middle, behind the 'B')

Captain Will Hubbard
DFC
From Leamington Spa, Warwickshire, born 25 February 1895.
Died Carlton, Victoria, Australia, 1 July 1969
3 Squadron
10 victories

Lieutenant William Edwin Jenkins
Born Rushden, 9 July 1898. KIFA France, 23 November 1917
60 Squadron
10 victories

Lieutenant Alfred Koch
MC
Born Grandbunten, Switzerland, 25 January 1894. Died Vancouver, in the 1980s
Alberta Dragoons; 1 & 6 (Obs), 50HD & 70 Squadrons
10 victories
(Koch is on the right, while on the left is H.K. Boyson (5))

Flight Sub-lieutenant John Joseph Malone
DSO
Canadian, born in the USA, 20 December 1894. KIA France, 30 April 1917
3 Wing & 3 Sqn RNAS
10 victories

Captain Alfred Edwin McKay
MC
Born Ontario, Canada, 27 December 1892. KIA France, 28 December 1917
24 & 23 Squadrons
10 victories

Captain Finlay McQuistan
DFC
From Greenock, Scotland
3 HH Bde, Royal Field Artillery; 12, 55 & 19 Squadrons
10 victories
(The aeroplane is an SE5a)

Captain Guy Borthwick Moore
MC
From Vancouver, Canada, born 28 May 1895. KIA France, 7 April 1918
1 Squadron
10 victories
(Moore is seated in a Nieuport Scout)

Sergeant Gordon Percy Olley
MM
Born Harleston, Norfolk, 29 April 1893. Died Wimbledon, 18 March 1958
Royal Fusiliers; 1 Squadron
10 victories

Captain John de Campbourne Paynter
DSC
Born Southsea, Hampshire, 17 May 1898. DoW Bergues airfield, 18 June 1918
6, 9, 10, 13 Sqns RNAS, 213 Sqn RAF
10 victories

Captain Arthur Clunie Randall
DFC
From Bothwell, Lanarkshire, born 6 February 1895
10th & 1st Border Rgts; 32 & 85 Squadrons
10 victories

Lieutenant Herbert Bolton Redler
MC
From Moorresburg, South Africa, born 27 January 1897. KIFA Tewksbury, 21 June 1918
28th London Rgt; 40 & 24 Squadrons
10 victories
(Redler is on the left, with R.N. Hall MC (5), E.L. Bath and W.A. Bond DSO MC (5))

Captain Harry Noel Cornforth Robinson
MC CdG(F)
From West Hartlepool, born 25 December 1898
46 & 70 Squadrons
10 victories

Lieutenant Indra Lal Roy
DFC
Born Calcutta, India, 2 December 1892. KIA France, 22 July 1918
56 & 40 Squadrons
10 victories

Captain Reginald Howard Rusby
DFC
From Redland, Bristol, born London, 4 September 1893
4th Gloster Rgt; 22 (Obs) & 29 Squadrons
10 victories

Captain Alfred Seymour Shepherd
DSO
From New South Wales, Australia, born 13 April 1893. KIA France, 20 July 1917
30th & 46th Battns. AIF; 29 Squadron
10 victories

Captain St.Cyprian Churchill Tayler
MC
Born Winchester, Hants, 26 February 1896. KIA France, 17 March 1918
Royal Sussex Rgt; 32 & 80 Squadrons
10 victories

Lieutenant Frank Harold Taylor
MC
From Toronto, born 11 August 1896. Died Long Island, NY, USA, 7 June 1985
204th & 116th Battns. CEF; 41 & 84 Squadrons
10 victories

Captain John Henry Tudhope
MC*
Born Johannesburg, South Africa, 17 April 1891. Died London, Ontario, 12 October 1956
South African Army; 40 Squadron
10 victories

Captain Stanley Harry Wallage
MC
Born Ipswich, Suffolk, 24 July 1895
7th Suffolk Rgt; 22 Squadron
10 victories
(Wallage is the pilot smoking a cigarette)

Captain William Lewis Wells
MC*
From Hounslow, Middx, born 1895. DoW France, 6 May 1918
8th Middlesex Rgt; 22 & 48 Squadrons
10 victories

Lieutenant Russell Winnicott
MC
Born Plymouth, Devon, 24 May 1898. KIFA France, 6 December 1917
41 Squadron
10 victories

Captain Thomas Colville-Jones (NO PHOTO)
From Buenos Aires, South American, born 1 November 1897. DoW/PoW France, 24 May 1918
20 & 48 Squadrons
11 victories

Captain Frederick John Gibbs (NO PHOTO)
MC*
Born Walsall, Staffordshire, 8 September 1894
South Staffordshire Rgt; 23 & 64 Squadrons
11 victories

Lieutenant Thomas Montagu Harries (NO PHOTO)
DFC
Born Tobago, British West Indies, 16 October 1889
45 (Obs) & 24 Squadrons
11 victories

Captain Geoffrey Herbert Hooper (NO PHOTO)
MC DFC
Born Sydney, Australia, 15 April 1891
Royal Engineers; 11 & 20 Squadrons
11 victories

Lieutenant Sydney Arthur Oades (NO PHOTO)
MC
Born New Cross, SE London, 27 September 1890
Royal Engineers; 22 Squadron
11 victories

Captain Cecil Christian Clark (NO PHOTO)
From Norwich, born 1898. Died 30 November 1939, buried Gosport, Hants
Royal Field Artillery; 1 Squadron
10 victories

Captain William Hastings Farrow (NO PHOTO)
DFC
From Cheadle Hume, Cheshire, born 30 March 1893
Royal Engineers; 47 & 64 Squadrons
10 victories

Captain Ronald Roscoe Thornley (NO PHOTO)
DSC
Born Cambridge, 10 July 1889
RNVR Armoured Car Sqn; 8 Sqn RNAS
10 victories

Name	Born/From	Sqn(s)	Fate
9 Victories			
Lt C H Arnison MC DFC	Gloucestershire, Eng	62	
Maj H H Balfour MC* CdG(F)	Camberley, Surrey	43	Died Sep 1988
Lt R G Bennett	Hanwell, Mx, England	20	KIA 28 May 18
Lt J A W Binnie	Glasgow, Scotland	48	Died 1962
Capt J D Breakey DFC*	Sheffield, England	3N,203	Died 1966
Capt F J S Britnall DSC DFC	High Wycombe, Bucks	3N,203	
Lt W H Brown MC	Victoria, BC, Canada	84	Died 28 Feb 69
Capt G W Bulmer MC	Dixon, Illinois, USA (British)	22	Died 1987
Flt Cdr F D Casey DSC	Clonmee, Ireland	3N	KIFA 11 Aug 17
Lt R D Coath	Maidenhead, England	48,11	Died 1967
Maj A T Cole MC DFC	Melbourne, Australia	2 AFC	Died 1966
Capt E D Cummings DFC	Franklin, Tasmania	2 AFC	
Capt D C Cunnell MC	Norwich, England	20	
Capt H C Daniel MC AFC	Senekal, OFS, S Africa	43	Died post 1945
Capt R J Dawes DFC	Lachine, Quebec, Canada	45,28	Died 22 Apr 83
Capt R A Del'Haye DFC CdG(B)	French, Br Subject 1914	19	KIFA 18 Nov 44
Capt G C Dixon	Vancouver, Canada	43,85,40	Died Feb 73
Capt J E Doyle DFC	Cleveden, Somerset	56,60	
Maj C Draper DSC	Liverpool, England	3W,6N,8N	Died Jan 79
Capt A T Drinkwater DFC	Queenscliff, Victoria	57,40	
F/Lt D F Fitzgibbon DSC	Hampstead, N London	10N	
Capt J H Forman DFC	Kirkfield, Ontario	6N,1N,201,70	Died '70
Lt F S Gordon DFC	Auckland, NZ	74	Died 27 Jun 85
Lt R M Gordon DFC	Glasgow, Scotland	204	
Capt A G Goulding MC DFC	Manitoba, Canada	17,150	Died Apr 1951
Capt G H Hackwill MC	Devon, England	22,44,54	
Capt J D I Hardman DFC	Yorkshire, England	19	Died 2 Mar 82
Lt F J Hunt DFC	Whitchurch, Hampshire	74	
Lt R L Johns	Kilburn, NW London	8N,208	KIFA 11 Jul 18
Capt N C Jones DFC	Altrincham, Cheshire	28,45	
Capt H S Kerby DSC AFC	Calgary, Canada	9N,3N	Died 8 Jun 63
Lt L W King	Westcliffe-on-Sea, Essex	22	
Capt F M Kitto MC	Pontypridd, Wales	43,54	
Capt C S I Lavers DFC	St Albans, England	23,1	
Capt J L Leith	London, England	25,46	
Maj S H Long DSO MC	Aldershot, Hampshire	29,24	Died 1952
Capt C N Lowe MC DFC	Lincolnshire, England	11,24	Died 1985
Capt N Macmillan MC AFC	Carsphairn, Scotland	45	Died 5 Aug 76
Capt C J Marchant MC	London, England	46	Died 1960s
Lt R F S Mauduit MC	English	11	Died 1928
Maj R S Maxwell MC DFC	Cricklewood, N London	25,20,54	
Capt J S McDonald	Newlands, Glasgow	208	
Lt C McEvoy DFC	Cricklewood, N London	66	Died 12 Oct 53
Capt D M McGoun MC	Montreal, Canada	20,22	
Capt J T Milne MC	London, England	48	KIA 24 Oct 17
Lt B H Moody	Capetown, S Africa	1	
Maj R B Munday DSC	Plymouth, Devon	8N	
Capt C G D Napier MC DCM	London, England	48	KIA 15 May 18
Maj E W Norton DSC CdG(F/B)	Newton, N. Wales	6N	
Capt S C O'Grady MC	Dublin, Eire	23	Died 1970s
F/Lt E Pierce	York, England	9N,3N	
Capt F C Ransley DFC	Caversham, Berkshire	48	
Capt W E Reed DFC	Jarrow, Tyne	19,92	
Maj G R M Reid DSO MC*	Largs, Ayr, Scotland	25,20	Died May 1991
Capt W W Rogers MC	Alberton, Canada	1	Died 11 Jan 67
Capt H V Rowley	Crich, Derbeyshire	1N,201	
Capt E J Salter LdH Cdg(F)	Greenbank, Ontario	54	Died 23 Mar 59
Lt J H Siddall	St Helens, Lancashire	209	KIA 25 Jul 18
Lt C J Sims DFC	Bournemouth, England	213	
Lt R H Sloley	Cape Town, South Africa	56	KIA 1 Oct 17
Capt A N Solly	Harrogate, Yorkshire	23,20	KIFA 11 Aug 17
Lt A G A Spence	Toronto, Canada	1N,201	
Capt F D Travers DFC CdG(F)	London, England	17,150	
Capt G W Wareing DFC	Warrington, Lancashire	29	KIA 27 Oct 18
Lt K B Watson DFC	Ontario, Canada	70	Died 5 Mar 60
Capt T M Williams MC DFC	Transvaal, S Africa	65	Died 10 Jun 56
Lt A Williamson	Leek, Staffordshire	88	
8 Victories			
Capt A W Aldred MC*	Eccles, Lancashire	70,3	
Lt G F Anderson DFC	Natal, South Africa	88	
Lt G G Bailey DFC	Barnes, W London	43	
Capt B P H Beanlands MC	Victoria, BC, Canada	70,24	KIFA 8 May 18
Lt D W Beard MM	Cheshire, England	4,11	
Capt E L Benbow MC	Abbotsbury, Dorset	40,85	KIA 30 May 18
Capt H A R Biziou DFC	Hampshire, England	87	KIFA 14 Jul 19
Capt G H Blaxland	NSW, Australia	2AFC	Died 25 Aug 69
Capt C A Brewster-Joske MC	Fiji (Australian)	1,46	Died 1947
Capt E W Broadberry MC	London, England	56	Died 26 Dec 67
Capt A J Brown MC	Deal, Kent	24,23	
Capt J M Child MC	Leytonstone, N London	18,84	Killed 23 Aug 18
Lt E S T Cole MC	Bristol, England	60,1	
Capt J G Coombe	Grimsby, Lincolnshire	29	
Lt W B Craig DFC	Smith's Falls, Ontario	204	KIA 26 Sep 18
Lt J J Dawe	Hertfordshire, England	24	KIA 7 Jun 18
Capt J D De Pencier	Vancouver, Canada	19	KIFA 17 May 20
Maj R M Drummond DSO* MC	Perth, W Australia	67,111	KIFA 27 Mar 45
Capt G M Duncan DFC	Edinburgh, Scotland	60	
Lt W Durrand MC	Wick, Scotland	20	Died 12 Oct 39
Lt H R Eycott-Martin DFC	Norwood, England	66	
Capt A L Fleming MC	Toronto, Canada	111	Died 26 Jan 69
Capt C B Glynn DFC	Liverpool, England	56,74	
Maj E O Grenfell MC AFC	Southend, Essex	1,60	
Capt V E Groom DFC	London, England	20	Died Dec 1990
Capt R G Hammersley CdG(F)	Atherstone, Warwick	24	
Lt F G Harlock	Stamford, Lincolnshire	20	
Capt H G Hegarty MC	County Galway, Eire	60	
Capt A S Hemming DFC	Banbaury, Oxon	41	
Lt G R Hicks DFC	Toronto, Canada	74	
Capt I F Hind	Johannesburg, S Africa	40	KIA 12 Aug 18
Lt T S Horry DFC	Boston, Lincolnshire	92	

Capt R W Howard MC	Sydney, Australia	2AFC	DoW 22 Mar 18
Capt K W Junor MC	Toronto, Canada	56	KIA 23 Apr 18
Capt R K Kirkman MC	Southsea, Hampshire	20	
Capt A G Knight DSO MC	Bedford, England	24,29	KIA 20 Dec 16
Capt K M StC G Leask MC*	Southsea, Hampshire	84	Died 24 Apr 74
Capt C A Lewis MC	Birkenhead, Cheshire	56	Died Jan 1997
Maj G L Lloyd MC AFC	Rhodesia, South Africa	60,40	
Capt D Lloyd-Evans MC DFC	Wales	64	
Lt W M MacDonald DFC	Vancouver, Canada	66	
Lt R G Malcolm MC	Owen Sound, Ontario	25	
Lt G I D Marks	Toronto, Canada	23	Died 21 Oct 49
Lt E H Masters CdG	Coventry, England	45	KIFA 24 Dec 18
Capt H B Maund	Hampstead, London	10N,210	
Lt J A McCudden MC	Kent, England	25,84	KIA 18 Mar 18
Capt R McDonald	Nova Scotia, Canada	8N,208	KIA 8 May 18
Capt H Meintjes MC AFC	Colesburg, South Africa	60,56	
Capt H M Moody MC	Shropshire, England	45	KIFA 23 Apr 31
Maj G W Murlis-Green DSO* MC	London, England	17,44	
Lt K K Muspratt MC	Bournemouth, England	56	KIFA 19 Mar 18
Capt T W Nash DFC* CdG(F)	Littlehampton, Sussex	204	KIA 23 Oct 18
Capt E Olivier	Oudtshoorn, S Africa	19	
Lt E C Pashley	Yarmouth, Norfolk	24	KIFA 17 Mar 17
Capt A H Peck DSO MC*	India (British)	111	
Capt P B Prothero	Ayrshire, Scotland	24,56	KIA 26 Jul 17
Maj J B Quested MC CdG(F)	Cheriton, Kent	11	Died 11 Mar 48
Lt-Col L W B Rees VC MC	Caernarvon, Wales	11,32	Died 28 Sep 55
Capt W T V Rooper CdG(B)	Gresford, England	1	DoW 9 Oct 17
Capt W J Rutherford	Montreal, Canada	60	
Capt H L Satchell	Rugby, England	20	Died 8 Jun 83
Capt F G Saunders MC*	Swansea, S Wales	47,17	
Lt C H Sawyer	Surbiton, Surrey	46	KIFA 8 Oct 18
Capt O J F Scholte MC	Hampstead, N London	48,60	OAS 30 Jul 18
Lt H W Sellars MC	Liverpool, England	11	KIA 15 May 18
Flt Cdr J E Sharman DSC* CdG(F)	Oak Lake, Manitoba, Can	10N	KIA 22 Jul 17
Capt G G Simpson DSC	NW, London	8N,9N	
Lt J H Smith	Cambellford, Ontario	46	Died 1959
Capt J K Summers MC	Birmingham, England	209	
Capt T C Traill DFC	Argentina, S America	20	Died 1970s
Lt A G Vlasto	Bracknell, Berkshire	46	Died 1 Mar 35
Lt J W Warner DFC	Boston Spa, Yorkshire	85	KIA 4 Oct 18
Lt C M Wilson DFC	Vancouver, Canada	29	KIA 14 Oct 18
Capt W A Wright CdG(B)	Frisby, Leicestershire	45	Died 26 Apr 90

7 Victories

Lt F Alberry DCM	Hobart, Tasmania	2AFC	Died 1969
Capt C P Allen	Liverpool, England	204	
Lt T H Barkell DFC	Sydney, Australia	4AFC	
Lt J C Bateman	Essex, England	1	
Capt A D Bell-Irving MC* CdG	Vancouver, Canada	7,60	Died 24 Apr 65
Lt W H Bland CdG(F)	Newbury, Berkshire	65	
Capt L Campbell	Hamilton, Canada	62	KIA 9 Oct 18
Lt L H T Capel	Hackney, London	20	
Lt R N Chandler DFC	Layton, N London	73	
Maj C M B Chapman MC	Canterbury, Kent	24,29	DoW 1 Oct 17
F/Lt W H Chisam	Carlisle, England	3N	
Capt A Claydon DFC	Lincolnshire, England	32	KIA 8 Jul 18
Capt S Cockerell	Osterley, Middx	24,151	
Lt A G Cooper CdG(F)	Essex, England	28	KIFA 29May 28
Capt S E Cowan MC**	Dublin, Eire	24,29	KIA 8 Nov 17
Capt E D Crundall DFC	Dover, England	8N,210	
Capt A S Cunningham-Reid DFC	London, England	85	Died 26 Mar 77
Lt R H Daly DSC	Leigh-on-Sea, Essex	10N,47	KIFA 1923
Capt E E Davies DFC	Kerang, Vic., Australia	2 AFC	Died 1969
Lt E F H Davis	Oxbow, Canada	41	
Lt P M Dennett	Southsea, Hampshire	8N,208	KIA 2 Jun 18
Lt J H Dewhirst DFC	Yorkshire, England	45	
Lt H E Dolan MC	Ealing, W London	74	KIA 11 May 18
Lt T A Doran	Essex, England	23	
Capt H F S Drewitt MC	Christchurch, NZ	23	Died 4 Jan 27
Lt C G Edwards DFC	St Albans, England	209	KIA 27 Aug 18
Lt H E O Ellis MC	London, England	40	
Lt R W Farquhar	Dulwich, SE London	18,32	KIA 30 Oct 18
Capt C McA G Farrell DFC	Smith's Falls, Canada	24	Died 31 Jan 88
Lt G B Foster DFC	Montreal, Canada	24	Died 3 Jun 74
Capt M M Freehill DFC		46,80	
Capt W B Green DFC	Stoke on Trent	32	
Lt F V Hall	Muswell Hill, N London	10N,210	KIA 15 May 18
Lt H H Hartley	Edinburgh, Scotland	48	KIA 14 Mar 18
Maj L G Hawker VC DSO	Longparish, Hampshire	6	KIA 23 Nov 16
Capt I H D Henderson MC	Chelsea, S London	19,56	KIFA 21 Jun 18
Capt W C Hilborn DFC	Alexandria, BC, Canada	66,28	DoI 26 Aug 18
Lt P K Hobson MC	Fleet, Lincolnshire	84	
Lt N W Hustings	England	19	Killed Apr 1923
Lt A E DeM Jarvis DFC CdG(F)	Napanee, Ont. Canada	17,150	Died 20 Jan 69
Capt L W Jarvis	London, England	56	
Lt A Jerrard VC	Lewisham, S London	66	Died 14 May 68
Lt A L Jones	Warwickshire, England	10N,210	
Capt G Jones DFC	Rushworth, Vic., Australia	4AFC	Died 24 Aug 92
Maj H W G Jones MC	Llandudno, Wales	32	
Lt H W Joslyn	Sintaluta, Saskatchewan	20	KIA 17 Aug 17
Lt E P Kenney DFC	Trafalgar, Vic., Australia	1AFC	
Capt A S G Lee MC	Nottingham, England	46	Died 21 May 75
Capt A A Leitch MC DFC	Manitoba, Canada	65	Died 31 Dec 54
Lt H O MacDonald	Cape Town, South Africa	84	KIFA WW2
Flt Cdr N M MacGregor DSC	London, England	6N,10N	
Capt J Mackereth	Fobbing, Essex	28,66	
Capt W Maclanachan		40	Died 1960s
Lt M P MacLeod DFC CdG(B)	Arnprior, Ontario, Can	41	Died Feb 1960
Capt H H Maddocks MC	London, England	54	
Lt R K McConnell DFC	Canada	46	
Lt P A McDougall MC	Scalloway, Shetland Is	24	
Lt P J McGinness DFC DCM	Framlingham, Vic., Aust	1 AFC	Died 25 Jan 55
Capt E T Morrow DFC	Toronto, Canada	62	
Capt W J B Nel	Transvaal, S African	84	

Capt C W Odell	Newport, Isle of Wight	46	
Capt A H Orlebar	Poddington, Beds	19,73,43	DOAS 1943
Lt R J Owen	Gosport, Newcastle	43	
F/Lt J A Page	Brockville, Ontario, Can	10N	KIA 22 Jul 17
Lt A J Palliser	Launceston, Tasmania	4AFC	KIA 4 Nov 18
Capt W D Patrick	Ayreshire, Scotland	1	
Capt W R G Pearson	S London, England	32	KIFA 20 Jun 18
Lt G C Peters DFC	Adelaide, W Australia	1AFC	
Capt S H Pratt	Sevenoaks, Kent	46	Died
Lt J C Preston	Bedford, England	150	
Maj S W Price MC	London, England	11	
2/Lt W T Price MC	Finchley, N London	48	Died 17 Jan 82
Lt S A Puffer	Olds, Alberta, Canada	41	Died 13 Jun 82
Lt L H Ray	Toronto, Canada	19	
Capt L L Richardson MC	Bereen Barraba, NSW	25	KIA 13 Apr 17
Capt J M Robb DFC	Hexham, Northumberland	32,92	Died 18 Dec 68
Capt H J T Saint DSC	Ruabon, N Wales	10N	
Lt D A Savage MC	Oxford, England	62	
Lt H Scandrett	London, England	25,11	
Lt K G Seth-Smith	England	70	KIFA 11 Aug 42
Capt L H Slatter DSC* DFC	Durban, South Africa	13N,213	Died 14 Apr61
Lt E A L F Smith	Victoria, BC, Canada	45	
Lt F C Stanton DCM CdG	Newport Pagnell, Bucks	22	
Capt C R Steele DFC	Lincoln, England	48	
Lt C O Stone	Chingford, Essex	2AFC	
Capt G J Strange	Dorset, England	40	KIA 24 Sep 18
Lt C L Stubbs	Liverpool, England	84	
Capt O M Sutton MC	Tunbridge Wells, Kent	54	KIFA 16 Aug 21
Capt A G V Taylor	England	20	KIA 17 Oct 17
Lt M S Taylor CdG(F)	Regina, Saskatchewan	9N,209	KIA 7 Jul 18
Capt D M Tidmarsh MC	Limerick, Eire	24,48	DOAS WW2
Lt N C Trescowthick DFC	Melbourne, Australia	4AFC	
Maj A M Vaucour MC* DFC	Upper Norwood, S London	70,45	Killed 16 Jul 18
2/Lt S R P Walter	Maidstone, Kent	32	KIFA 31 Jul 18
Lt H J Walkerdine MC	Rowditch, Derbyshire	56	Died 18 Jun 66
Lt J J Wellwood DFC	Drouin, Vic., Australia	2AFC	
Capt H G White	Maidstone, Kent	20,29	Died 23 Sep 83
Capt P Wilson MC	Cheshire, England	28	

6 Victories

Capt J V Aspinall	London, England	22,11	KIA 15 May 18
Lt J L Barlow	Wivenhoe, Essex	40	KIA 23 Sep 17
Lt N S Boulton	Westbury, Wiltshire	20	KIA 29 Sep 18
Lt P Boulton DFC	Stoke on Trent, England	210	
Lt C G Brock	Southsea, Hampshire	1N,209,3	Died 20Feb67
Capt E G Brookes DFC	Bromsgrove, England	65	
Lt J C Bush MC	Dorset, England	22	KIA 7 Oct 17
Capt W J Cairnes	Drogheda, Eire	19,74	
Lt J G S Candy DFC	Hampshire, England	19	
Capt H G Clappison	Hamilton, Canada	204	Died 15 May 77
Capt E D Clarke MC	Reading, England	45	Died 5 Sep 66
Lt H G Clements	Chilham, Kent, England	74	Died 6 May 83
Lt J H Colbert	Llangollen, N Wales	20	
Lt H N Compton DFC	Winnipeg, Canada	23	Died 1951
Lt R E Conder	Norwood, SE London	20	
Capt G K Cooper	Catford, SE London	8N,208	
Capt M L Cooper DFC	Bournemouth/Dublin	213	KIA 2 Oct 18
Lt E F Crabb DFC	Delhi, Ontario, Canada	92	
FSL T G Culling DSC	Auckland, New Zealand	1N	KIA 8 Jun 17
Capt W G S Curphy MC*	Hampstead, London	32	KIA 14 May 17
Lt J E A R Daly DFC	Jamaica, BWI	24	KIFA 3 Jul 18
Capt H B Davey	Camberley, Surrey	25,11	
Lt C R Davidson MC	Poona, India	14,111	
Capt H G W Debenham	Essex, England	46,208	
Capt J E Drummond	Ontario, Canada	48	Died 29 Jan 79
Flt Cdr C A Eyre	Derbyshire, England	1N	KIA 7 Jul 17
Capt W S Fielding-Johnson MC*	Leicester, England	56	Died 10 Feb 53
Lt J P Findlay	Cape Town, South Africa	88	
Lt A W Franklyn MC	Hounslow, W London	3	
Capt D M B Galbraith DSC*	Carlton Place, Ontario	1W,8N	Killed 29 Mar21
Capt G C Gardiner DFC LdH CdG	Poonah, India	47,150	
Lt R C D'A Gifford	Brierley Heath, Staffs	208	Died Oct 1991
Capt G H D Gossip	Sydney, Australia	4N,204	Died 1922
Capt D W Grinnell-Milne MC DFC	Beckenham, Kent	56	Died Nov 1973
Lt A J Haines DFC	Evesham, Worcester	45	KIA 10 Aug 18
Capt J P Hales	Guelph, Ontario	9N,203	KIA 23 Aug 18
Capt R N Hall MC	Natal, South Africa	40	
Capt H J Hamilton MC	London, England	1,29	KIFA 13 Jun 18
Lt L Hamilton DFC	Crowborough, Sussex	17,150	KIFA 1927
FSL G W Hemming DSC CdG	Worcester, England	4N,204	
Lt R A Hewat	Lawrence, Mass., (Can)	19,87	KIA 14 Aug 18
Capt W G R Hinchcliffe DFC AFC	Liverpool, England	10N,210	KIFA Mar 28
Capt F H Hudson MC	Beckenham, Kent	54	DOAS 6 Jun 22
Capt T V Hunter	London, England	66	KIFA 5 Dec 17
Maj V H Huston MC	Ireland	18	
Flt Cdr P A Johnston	Sydney, Australia	8N	KIA 17 Aug 17
2/Lt E T S Kelly	Picton, Ontario, Canada	1	KIA 13 Jun 18
Lt G E B Lawson DFC	Cape Town, S Africa	32	KIFA 19 Nov 22
Maj M LeBlanc-Smith DFC	Leatherhead, Surrey	73	Died 29 Oct 86
Lt G A Lingham DFC	Melbourne, Australia	43	
Capt A T Loyd	Hawkhurst, Kent	25,32	KIA 28 Sep 17
Capt T C Luke MC	St Judes, Plymouth, Eng	60,209	DOAS 1935
Capt G F Malley MC	Sydney, Australia	4AFC	
Lt M J J G Mare-Montembault MC		32	
Lt W T Martin	Kandy, Ceylon	22	
Capt F H M Maynard AFC	Waiuku, New Zealand	1N	
Lt M McCall	Ayr, Scotland	20	
Lt R W McKenzie MC	Adelaide, S Australia	2AFC	Died 1945
Capt R McLaughlin DFC	Belfast, N Ireland	201	
Lt O L McMaking	Southsea, Hampshire	45	KIA 11 Sep 17
Capt E S Meek	Sandford, Ontario, Can	29	
Lt G W Meggitt MC	Newport, S Wales	25,22	KIA 8 Nov 17
Lt A W B Miller	Staffordshire, England	29	KIA 13 Jul 17
Capt N C Millman	Toronto, Canada	48	Died 27 Jul 81

F/Lt G E Nash	Stoney Creek, Canada	10N	Died 10 Apr 76
Lt A Paget DFC	Wiltshire, England	66	
Capt G A H Pidcock CdG(F)		60,73	Died Feb 1976
Lt S L G Pope	Dublin, Eire	60	
Lt W A Pritt MC	Leamington Spa, England	66	
Lt T G Rae DFC	Glasgow, Scotland	48	
Maj R Raymond-Barker MC	Bisley, Gloucestershire	48,11	KIA 20 Apr 18
Lt A Rice-Oxley DFC	Watford, Herts	45	
Capt H A Rigby	Melbourne, Australia	1	
Capt T S Sharpe DFC	Gloucester, England	73	
Lt D E Smith	Dundee, Scotland	20	KIA 14 Aug 18
Lt C R Smythe	Hampton, Middx	11	
Maj W V Strugnell MC*	St Denys, Southampton	1,54	Died 1977
Maj R N M Stuart-Wortley MC	Highcliffe Castle, Hamps	22	Died 1920
Lt W K Swayze	Toronto, Canada	62	Died 1920
Capt R Sykes DFC	Stockton-on-Tees, Eng	9N,203,210	Died 1970s
Capt H L Symons	Toronto, Canada	65	Died 17 May 62
Capt G P Taylor MC	Mosman, Sydney, Aust.	66	Died Dec 1966
Lt C R Thompson DFC	Mossel Bay, South Africa	84	Died 16 Mar 73
Lt C R J Thompson	Melbourne, Australia	19	KIFA 17 Jul 18
Lt A V Tonkin DFC	Avenal, Vic. Australia	1 AFC	Died 17 Feb 69
F/Lt G L Trapp	New Westminster, Canada	10N	KIA 12 Nov 17
Lt P M Tudhope DFC	Orange Free State, SA	46	
Lt B A Walkerdine	Mansfield, Notts	64	
Lt H E Watson	St John's, Canada	41	Died 11 Sep 57
Capt W G Westwood	Pietermaritzberg, SA	88	
Lt W A Wheeler	Coventry, England	88	
Lt W O B Winkler	Edinburgh, Scotland	48	Died 24 Nov 52

5 Victories

Lt J A Aldridge	Twickenham, Middx	19	
FL G B Anderson	Ottawa, Canada	3N	
Capt D'U V Armstrong DFC	Durban, South Africa	60,151	KIFA 13 Nov 18
Maj A R Arnold DSC DFC CdG	Fareham, England	8N,79	
Lt F F Babbage DFC	Exeter, Devon	20	
Capt L D Baker	London, England	23	Died 26 Mar 71
Capt L D Bawlf	Winnipeg, Canada	3N,203	Died 22 Aug 66
Maj G G Bell	London, England	10,41	KIFA 29 Jul 18
Lt R M Bennett	Beckenham, Kent, Eng	204	KIA 28 Sep 18
Lt R C Berlyn	Birmingham, England	3N,203	
Capt F Billinge DFC	London, England	20,32,56	Died 1928
Lt A W Blake	Transvaal, South Africa	19	KIFA 14 Dec 22
Lt A V Blenkiron	Patrington, E Yorks	25,56,151	
Capt W O Boger DFC	Winnipeg, Canada	11,56	KIA 10 Aug 18
Capt W A Bond DSO MC*	Leicester, England	40	KIA 22 Jul 17
Lt E B Booth	Toronto, Canada	70	KIFA 7 Apr 18
Capt A J Bott MC*	Stoke on Trent, England	70,111	Died 1952
Lt F S Bowles	Surrey, England	45	
Lt G Bremridge AFC	Devon, England	65	
Capt O C Bridgeman MC	Shropshire, England	80	Died 21 Dec 31
Capt A R Brown DFC	Launceston, Tasmania	1 AFC	Died 1964
Lt M G S Burger DFC	Graaff Sennett, S Africa	54	
Maj J C Callaghan MC	Co. Dublin, Eire	18,87	KIA 2 Jul 18
2/Lt D E Cameron	Hythe, Sussex	1	
Capt R M Charley MC CdG(F)	England	54	Died 1986
Lt J E Child	Belmont, Surrey	45	Died 3 Nov 18
Capt A G Clark	Sydney, Australia	2 AFC	Died 26 Dec 60
Lt G J Cox	Carlton, Australia	2 AFC	
Capt G M Cox MC	Calcutta, India	65	
Capt K Crawford	Wandsworth, SW London	24,60	KIA 11 Apr 18
Capt G B Crole MC	Edinburgh, Scotland	40,43	Died 3 Mar 65
Capt J B Crompton	Montreal, Canada	60	Died 1980s
Lt R J Cullen	Edinburgh, Scotland	88	
Capt L Cummings	Ottawa, Canada	1	Died 21 Dec 55
Capt F J Cunninghame	Northampton, England	48	
Capt S Dalrymple DFC	Melbourne, Australia	27,139	
Maj C J W Darwin DSO	Durham, England	27,87	DOAS Dec 41
Flt Cdr M J G Day DSC	St Ives, Hunts, England	13N	KIA 27 Feb 18
Lt P A DeFontenay	Mauritius	29	
Maj B P H De Roeper AFC	Forest Gate, London	6N	
Capt E B Drake	Pembroke, S Wales	209	KIA 29 Sep 18
Maj C S Duffus OBE MC	Halifax, Canada	22	
Lt E C Eaton	Montreal, Canada	65	KIA 26 Jun 18
Capt H J Edwards	Victoria, Australia	32	Died 10 Sep 67
Lt H W Elliott MC	London, England	48	KIFA 5 Jun 18
FSL S E Ellis	Kingston, Ontario	4N	KIFA 12 Jul 17
2/Lt H C Evans DSO	Camberley, Surrey	24	KIA 3 Sep 16
Maj E L Foot	Essex, England	11,60	KIFA 23 Jun 23
Lt H H S Fowler	Toronto, Canada	8N	Died 26 Jan 62
Lt G W G Gauld DFC	Toronto, Canada	74	Died 28 Oct 64
Lt D H S Gilbertson	Hertford, England	70	KIA 4 Sep 18
Lt W B Giles	Bristol, Avon	74	Died 1990s
Lt W J Gillespie CdG(F)	Alberta, Canada	41	
Capt M E Gonne MC	SW London, England	54	KIA 8 Aug 18
Lt H B Good	Taplow, Bucks	92	KIA 5 Sep 18
Lt H A F Goodison	Highgate, London	23	
Capt K L Gopsill	Handsworth, England	23,43	KIFA 15 Feb 18
Maj R Graham DSO DSC* DFC	Japan (Scottish)	13N,213	Died 1967
F/Lt E R Grange DSC	Michigan, USA (Canadian)	1W,8N	Died 13 Jul 88
Lt W E Gray DFC	Berwick on Tweed	213	
Sgt J H R Green It Bronze Medal	Buckland, Berkshire	25	KIFA 15 Dec 17
Capt E Gribben MC	County Down, Ireland	70	
Capt J E Hallonquist DFC	Mission City, BC, Canada	28	Died 22 Aug 58
Capt E McN Hand DFC	Ontario, Canada	45	Died 19 Mar 54
Maj A T Harris AFC	Cheltenham, Glos	45	Died 6 Apr 84
Capt H A Hay MC	Bath, Somerset	11	
Lt R B Hay MC	Wiltshire, England	48	KIA 17 Jul 17
Lt E S Headlam	Nant, Tasmania	1AFC	
Lt P F C Howe	Swaziland, S Africa	74	
Capt D J Hughes DFC	Hoole, Chester	3	
Capt E Y Hughes	Brigend, South Wales	46,3	
Lt C E Hurst	Leicester, England	22	
Capt G A Hyde MC	Easingwold, Yorkshire	54	
Lt A G Jarvis	Suffolk, England	28	

Lt C H Jeffs	Grimsby, Lincolnshire	56	
Lt K J P Laing	Hawick, Scotland	1	
Lt D Langlands	Orpington, Kent	23	
Capt J D Latta MC	Hendon, London	1,60	
Capt F H Laurence MC	London, England	70	
Lt J S Lennox	Glasgow, Scotland	66	
Lt J D Lightbody	Hamilton, Scotland	204	KIA 4 Nov 18
Lt E Lindup MC	South Africa	20	
Lt R H Little	Eden, Ontario, Canada	48	Died 10 Sep 92
2/Lt C G O MacAndrew	Ayr, Scotland	11	KIA 2 Oct 17
Lt R M MacDonald	Winnipeg, Canada	87	Died 29 Aug 60
Capt L J MacLean MC*	Ealing, West London	41	
Lt J F N MacRae	Beaverton, Ontario, Can	23	
2/Lt P S Manley	Thorld, Ont, Canada	62	Died 30 Oct 52
Capt L M Mansbridge	Willesden Green, London	1,23	Died 1993
Lt W S Mansell	Wimbledon, S London	22,1	KIA 11 Sep 17
2/Lt W H Maxted	Hemel Hempstead, Herts	3	KIFA 17 Dec 18
Maj R StC McClintock MC		64	KOAS Jun 22
Capt J H McNearney DFC	Jarvis, Ontario, Canada	79	DOAS 1 Mar 19
Lt R F McRae	Niagara Falls, Canada	46	Died 16 May 92
Lt H W Medlicott	London, England	2	Shot 21 May 18
Capt F J W Mellersh	London, England	9N,209	KIFA 1950s
Lt K C Mills	London, England	1	KIA 8 Aug 18
Lt H A S Molyneaux DFC	Toronto, Canada	56	Died 30 Jan 85
Capt J T Morgan	Willesden, N London	70	KIFA 29 Oct 18
Capt W J Mostyn	Liverpool, England	22	
Capt H E Mott	Winnipeg, Canada	9N	
Col R H Mulock DSO*	Winnipeg, Canada	1W	Died 23 Jan 61
Lt H C M Nangle	Salisbury, Rhodesia	62	
Capt R H G Neville MC	Cricklewood, London	23	
Lt T H Newsome	Dewsbury, Yorkshire	22	
Capt T A Oliver	Loughborough, England	1,29	KIA 14 Aug 17
Lt E E Owen	Ham, Surrey	1	
Lt C S Paul DFC	Thanis, New Zealand	1AFC	Died 22 Jan 19
Capt E R Pennell DFC	London, England	27,84	
Lt E H Peverell	Ilkley, Yorkshire	70	
Maj C E M Pickthorn MC	Suffolk, England	32,84	Died 3 Mar 38
Lt G Pilditch MC	Pretoria, South African	73	
Lt G R Poole	Bradford, W Yorkshire	88	
Maj F J Powell MC	Patricroft, Lancashire	5	Died 1980s
Lt H J Pratt	Gunnesbury, W London	48	
Capt J W Rayner	Gateshead, Tyne	60	
Lt G P S Reid MC	Tenerife, Canary Islands	20	KIFA 16 Oct 17
Lt A I Riley AFC	Wimbledon, S London	48	
Lt N Roberts DFC MM	Broughton, Manchester	48	
Maj W D S Sanday DSO MC	Liverpool, England	2,70,19	
Capt R H M S Saundby MC	Birmingham, England	24,41	Died 25 Sep 71
Lt-Col A J L Scott MC	Christchurch, NZ	60	DOAS Jan 22
Capt J P Seabrook	Cape Town, South Africa	11	
Lt F Sharpe	London, England	1	
Capt E L Simonson	Melbourne, Australia	2AFC	
Lt W A Smart	Cardiff, S Wales	1	
Lt H C Smith	Leamington Spa, Warks	213	
Capt S P Smith	Aldershot, Hampshire	6,46	KIA 6 Apr 18
Capt J G S C Smith-Grant	Glenlivet, Scotland	70,28	Died 29 May 18
Capt N R Smuts DFC	Johannesburg, SA	3	
Lt W H Sneath	Hendon, N London	8N,208	KIA 6 Apr 18
Lt I O Stead	Kimberley, South Africa	22	
Sgt T F Stephenson DCM	Peterborough, England	11	KIA 20 Nov 17
Capt F D Stevens OBE	Bury St Edmunds, Suffolk	20	
Capt O Stewart MC AFC	London, England	54	Died 1976
Capt M Thomas		41	Died 20 May 84
Flt Cdr H G Travers DSC	Kensington, London	3N	
Lt J S Turnbull	Darlinghurst, NSW, Aust	56,41	KIA 17 Jun 18
Lt A H Turner	Birmingham, England	213	
Lt K M Walker	Nora de Gaya, Portugal	209	KIA 12 Aug 18
Lt J W Wallwork MC	Radcliffe, Nr Manchester	40	DoI 18 Dec 22
Lt G A Welsh	Sunderland, Ontario	210	Died 16 Feb 65
2/Lt M S West	Shawcross, Hampshire	11	KIA 11 Nov 17
Capt L E Whitehead	London, England	60,65	KIA 20 May 18
Lt R K Whitney	Quebec, Canada	60	Died 1983
Lt E G H C Williams	Birmingham, England	48	
Lt F J Williams	Scarborough, Yorks	29	
Lt C F C Wilson	Newport, S Wales	84	
Flt Cdr R R Winter	Woodside Park, London	6N,9N	KIA 3 Feb 18
Capt J H G Womersley MC	Yeaton, Shropshire	43	
Maj H A Wood MC	Toronto, Canada	24	Died 28 Aug 59
Capt C H C Woollven	Plymouth, Devon	25	
Lt C E Worthington	Leicester, England	87	
Lt V M Yeates	W Dulwich, London	46	Died 15 Dec 34
2/Lt G C Young	Perth, Scotland	60	
Capt E L Zink	Kilburn, N London	18,32	

Captain Edward Vernon Rickenbacker
MoH, DSC (9 OLCs) LdH(F) CdG(F)
Born Columbus, Ohio, 8 October 1890. Died Zurich, Switzerland, 27 July 1973
94th Aero Squadron
26 victories

Captain Frederick Warrington Gillet
DFC* CdG(B)
Born Baltimore, Maryland, 28 November 1895. Died 21 December 1969
79 Squadron RAF
20 victories

Captain Howard Albert Kullberg
DFC
Born West Somerville, Massachusetts, 10 September 1896
1 Squadron RAF
19 victories

Captain William Carpenter Lambert
DFC
Born Irontown, Ohio, 18 August 1894. Died Irontown, 19 March 1982
24 Squadron RAF
18 victories

1st Lieutenant Frank Luke Jr
MoH DSC* CdG Italian War Cross
Born Phoenix, Arizona, 19 May 1897. KIA France, 29 September 1918
27th Aero Squadron
18 victories

Captain August Thayer Iaccaci
DFC
Born Hingham, Massachusetts, 6 June 1893. Died Madison, Connecticut, 30 April 1980
20 Squadron
17 victories

Captain Paul Thayer Iaccaci
DFC
Born Paris, France, 26 July 1890. Died Hanover, New Hampshire, 26 July 1965
20 Squadron
17 victories

Major Gervais Raoul Lufbery
LdH(F) MM(F) MM(Br) CdG & 10 Palmes (F) Montenegrin Medal for Military Valor, Purple Heart (1 May 2004)
Born 14 March 1885, Chamalieres, France. KIA France, 19 May 1918
VB106 Esc, N124 Esc, 94th Aero Squadron
16 victories

Captain Oran John Rose
DFC
From Platte County, Missouri, born 23 March 1893. Died Los Angeles, June 1971
92 Squadron RAF
16 victories

Captain Elliott White Springs
DSC DFC
Born Fort Hill, South Carolina, 31 July 1896. Died 15 October 1959
85 Sqn RAF, 148th Aero Sqn
16 victories

Captain Frederick Libby
MC
From Sterling, Colorado, born 15 July 1891. Died Los Angeles, 9 January 1970
23 (Obs), 11 (Obs), 43 & 25 Squadrons RFC/RAF
14 victories

Lieutenant Kenneth Russell Unger
DFC
Born Newark, New Jersey, 19 April 1898. Died Florida, 6 January 1979
210 Squadron RAF
14 victories

1st Lieutenant David Endicott Putnam
DSC LdH(F) MM(F) CdG(F)
Born Jamaica Plains, Massachusetts, 10 December 1898. KIA France, 12 September 1918
Spa94, MS156, Spa38 Escadrilles, 139th Aero USAS
13 victories

Captain George Augustus Vaughan Jr
DSC DFC
Born Dongan Hill, Brooklyn, NY, 20 May 1897. Died New York, 31 July 1989
84 Sqn RAF, 17th Aero Sqn
13 victories

1st Lieutenant Frank Leamon Baylies
LdH(F) MM(F) CdG(F)
Born Bedford, Massachusetts, 23 September 1895. KIA France, 17 June 1918
Spa73 & Spa3 Escadrilles
12 victories

Lieutenant Louis Bennett Jr
Born Weston, Virginia, 22 September 1894. KIA France, 24 August 1918
40 Squadron RAF
12 victories

Captain Field Eugene Kindley
DSC* DFC
Born Pea Ridge, Gravette, Arkansas, 13 March 1896. KIFA Texas, 1 February 1920
65 Sqn RAF, 148th Aero Sqn USAS
12 victories

Major Reed Gresham Landis
DSC DFC
Born Ottawa, Illinois, 17 July 1896. Died Arkansas, 30 May 1975
40 Sqn RAF, 25th Aero Sqn, and 4th Pursuit Group USAS
12 victories

Captain Frederick Ives Lord
DFC*
Born Manitowoc, Wisconsin, 8 April 1900. Murdered in Los Angeles, California, 21 July 1967
79 Squadron RAF
12 victories

Captain Clive Wilson Warman
DSO MC
Born Norfolk, West Virginia, 30 June 1892.
DoI (flying accident) Edmonton, Canada, 12 June 1919
Canadian Light Infantry; 23 Squadron RFC
12 victories

Captain Emile John Lussier
DFC
Born Chicago, Illinois, 10 October 1895. Died Westminster, Maryland, 11 December 1974
73 Squadron RAF
11 victories
(Lussier is seated in a Sopwith Camel)

Captain James William Pearson
DFC
Born Bridgeport, Connecticut, 2 April 1895. Died Nutley, New Jersey, 28 January 1993
23 Squadron RAF
11 victories

1st Lieutenant Lloyd Andrews Hamilton
DSC DFC
Born Troy, New York, 13 June 1894. KIA France, 24 August 1918
3 Sqn RAF, 17th Aero Sqn USAS
10 victories

1st Lieutenant Duerson Knight
Born Chicago, Illinois, 21 January 1893. Died California, June 1983
1 Squadron RAF
10 victories

Captain Oliver Colin LeBoutillier
From Montclair, New Jersey, born 24 May 1895. Died Las Vegas, Nevada, 12 May 1983
9 Sqn RNAS, 209 Sqn RAF
10 victories
(The aeroplane is a Sopwith Camel)

1st Lieutenant Jacques Michael Swaab
DSC
From Philadelphia, PA, born 21 April 1894. Died Los Angeles, 7 July 1963
22nd Aero Squadron USAS
10 victories

1st Lieutenant Paul Frank Baer
DSC* LdH(F) CdG(F)
From Fort Worth, Indiana, born 29 January 1895. KIFA, Hong Kong, 9 December 1930
Spa80 Escadrille, 103rd Aero Sqn USAS
9 victories

Captain Thomas Gantz Cassidy
DSC* LdH(F) CdG(F)
Born Waterloo, Iowa, 5 January 1896. Died Lake Forest, Illinois, 9 July 1972
Spa57, Spa163 Escadrilles, 28th Aero USAS
9 victories

1st Lieutenant Frank O'Driscoll Hunter
DSC(4 OLCs) LdH(F)
From Savannah, Georgia, born 8 December 1894. Died Savannah, 25 June 1982
94th & 103rd Aero Squadrons USAS
9 victories

Lieutenant Jens Frederick Larsen
From Waltham, Massachusetts, born 10 August 1891.
Died Winston Salem, North Carolina, May 1981
Canadian Field Artillery; 84 Squadron RAF
9 victories

1st Lieutenant Chester Ellis Wright
DSC*
Born Readville, Massachusetts, 1 September 1897
93rd Aero Squadron USAS
9 victories

1st Lieutenant Howard Burdick
DFC
Born Brooklyn, New York, 12 December 1891. Died Los Angeles, January 1975
17th Aero Squadron USAS
8 victories

Captain Alvin Andrew Callender
Born New Orleans, Louisiana, 4 July 1893. KIA France, 30 October 1918
32 Squadron RAF
8 victories

1st Lieutenant Henry Robinson Clay Jr
DSC DFC
Born Plattsburg, Missouri, 27 November 1895.
Died (influenza) Coblenz, Germany, 17 February 1919
43 Sqn RAF, 148th Aero Sqn USAS
8 victories

Captain Hamilton Coolidge
DSC CdG(F)
Born Brookline, Massachusetts, 1 September 1895. KIA France, 27 October 1918
94th Aero Squadron USAS
8 victories
(Coolidge is seated in a Nieuport Scout)

Lieutenant D'Arcy Fowlis Hilton
MC AFC
Born Youngstown, New York, 17 October 1889. Died October 1973
29 Squadron RFC
8 victories

2nd Lieutenant Clinton S Jones Jr
DSC*
From San Francisco, California, born 1 January 1892. Died Sacramento, CA, 23 June 1965
22nd Aero Squadron USAS
8 victories

Captain James Armand Meissner
DSC* CdG(F)
From New York, born Londonderry, Nova Scotia, born 20 July 1896. Died Birmingham, Alabama, 16 January 1936
94th & 147th Aero Squadrons USAS
8 victories

1st Lieutenant Edwin Charles Parsons
MM(F) CdG(F) Order of Leopold(B) CdG(B)
Born Holyoak, Massachusetts, 24 September 1892. Died Sarasota, Florida, 2 May 1968
N124 & Spa3 Escadrilles
8 victories

Lieutenant Walter Karl Simon
DFC
Born New Orleans, Louisiana, 14 September 1986. Died Kings Port, Tennessee, 16 May 1971
139 Squadron RAF
8 victories

1st Lieutenant Martinus Stenseth
DSC
Born Heiberg, Minnesota, 11 June 1890. Died Las Vegas, Nevada, 25 June 1979
28th Aero Squadron USAS
8 victories

1st Lieutenant Wilbert Wallace White Jr
DSC* CdG(F)
Born New York City, NY, 1 May 1889. KIA France, 10 October 1918
147th Aero Squadron USAS
8 victories

Major John Charles Biddle
DSC LdH(F) CdG(F) PH, Order of Leopold(B)
Born Andalusia, Pennsylvania, 13 May 1890. Died Andalusia, 22 March 1972
Spa73 & N124 Escadrilles, 103 & 13th Aero Sqns, & 4th PG USAS
7 victories

Major Reed McKinley Chambers
DSC(3 OLCs) LdH(F) CdG(F)
Born Onaga, Kansas, 18 August 1894. Died St Thomas, Virgin Islands, 16 January 1972
Tennessee National Guard; 94th Aero Squadron USAS
7 victories

Adjutant James Alexander Connelly Jr
DSC MM(F) CdG(F)
From Philadelphia, PA, born 1895. Died in New York, 2 February 1944
Spa157 & Spa163 Escadrilles
7 victories

Captain Harvey Weir Cook
DSC*
Born Wilkenson, Indiana, 1893. KOAS New Zealand, 25 March 1943
94th Aero Squadron USAS
7 victories

1st Lieutenant Jesse Orrin Creech
DFC
Born Harlan County, Kentucky, 22 August 1895. Died Louisville, Kentucky, 16 February 1948
148th Aero Squadron
7 victories

Captain John Owen Donaldson
DFC
Born Fort Yates, North Dakota, 14 May 1897. KIFA nr. Philadelphia, 7 September 1930
32 Squadron RAF
7 victories

Lieutenant John Sharpe Griffith
DFC
From Seattle, Washington, born 26 November 1898.
Died Rivermead, Long Island, 14 October 1974
60 Squadron RFC/RAF
7 victories

Captain Frank Lucien Hale
DFC
Born Syracuse, New York, 6 August 1895. Died Buffalo, NY, 7 June 1944
32 & 85 Squadrons RAF
7 victories

Lieutenant-Colonel Harold Evans Hartney
DSC LdH(F) CdG(F)
From Pakenham, Ontario, Canada, born 19 April 1888. Died Washington DC, 5 October 1947
105th Saskatchewan Fusiliers; 20 Sqn RFC, 27th Aero Sqn & 1st PG USAS
7 victories
(Generally listed among the American aces, he only became an American citizen in 1923)

1st Lieutenant Lancing Colton Holden Jr
DSC*
From New York, born 8 October 1896. KIFA nr. Sparta, Tennessee, 13 November 1938
95th Aero Squadron USAS
7 victories
(Holding is on the left, with Z.R. Miller (5))

Captain Gorman deFreest Larner
DSC* CdG(F)
Born Washington DC, 5 July 1897. Died Easton, Maryland, 20 May 1984
Spa86 Escadrille, 103rd Aero Sqn USAS
7 victories

1st Lieutenant Wendel Archibald Robertson
Born Oklahoma City, Oklahoma, 7 May 1894
139th Aero Squadron USAS
7 victories

1st Lieutenant Leslie J Rummell
DSC
From Newark, New Jersey, born 21 February 1895. Died (influenza) France, 2 February 1919
93rd Aero Squadron USAS
7 victories

1st Lieutenant Karl Schoen Jr
DSC
From Indianapolis, Indiana, 20 October 1896. KIA France, 29 October 1918
139th Aero Squadron USAS
7 victories
(Schoen stands in front of a Spad)

Captain Sumner Sewell
DSC LdH(F) CdG(F) Order of Leopold(B)
Born Bath, Maine, 17 June 1897. Died Bath, 26 January 1965
American Field Ambulance Service 1917, 95th Aero Squadron USAS
7 victories

Lieutenant Harold Albert White
DFC
From Schenectady, New York
23 Squadron RAF
7 victories

1st Lieutenant Hilbert Leigh Bair
DFC
From New York City, NY, born 15 November 1894.
Died White Springs, NY, 24 November 1985
24 Sqn RAF, 25th Aero Sqn USAS
6 victories

1st Lieutenant James Dudley Beane
DSC CdG(F)
Born New York City, NY, 20 January 1896. KIA France, 30 October 1918
Spa69 Escadrille, 22nd Aero USAS
6 victories

Captain Clayton Lawrence Bissell
DSC DFC
Born Kane, Pensylvania, 29 July 1896. Died Murfreesbro, Tennessee, 24 September 1972
148th Aero Squadron
6 victories

Lieutenant Charles Arthur Bissonette
From Los Angeles, CA, born 27 December 1895. Died Los Angeles, 27 April 1971
64 & 24 Squadrons RAF
6 victories

Captain Raymond Arthur Brooks
DSC SS
Born Framingham, Massachusetts, 1 November 1895. Died Summit, New Jersey, 17 July 1991
139th & 22nd Aero Squadrons USAS
6 victories

1st Lieutenant Douglas Campbell
DSC (4 OLCs) LdH(F) CdG(F)
From San Jose, nr. San Francisco, 7 June 1896.
Died Greenwich, Connecticut, 16 December 1990
94th Aero Squadron USAS
6 victories
(Campbell is standing by a Nieuport 28)

Lieutenant Charles Gray Catto
Born Dallas, Texas, 7 November 1896. Died Waco, Texas, 24 June 1972
45 Squadron RAF
6 victories

Captain Norman Cooper[+]
DFC
Born Schenectady, New York, 2 October 1888.
73 Squadron RAF
6 victories
([+] real name E.S. Tooker)

1st Lieutenant Edward Peck Curtis
DSC CdG(F)
From Rochester, New York, born 14 January 1897. Died Rochester, 13 March 1987
95th Aero Squadron USAS
6 victories

1st Lieutenant Murray Keith Guthrie
DSC**
Born Minneapolis, Minnesota, born 29 May 1896. Died in Texas in 1985
13th Aero Squadron USAS
6 victories

1st Lieutenant Frank Kerr Hays
DSC
From Louisville, Kentucky, born 3 November 1896. Died Carmel, California, 9 March 1988
13th Aero Squadron USAS
6 victories

1st Lieutenant Donald Hudson
DSC
Born Tapeka, Missouri, 21 December 1895. Died Fort Meade, Maryland, 11 June 1967
27th Aero Squadron USAS
6 victories

Lieutenant David Sinton Ingalls
DSC* DFC LdH(F)
Born Cleveland, Ohio, 28 January 1899. Died Hunting Valley, Ohio, 26 April 1985
US Navy Aviator; 213 Squadron RAF
6 victories

1st Lieutenant Howard Clayton Knotts
DSC DFC
From Carlinville, Illinois, born 25 August 1895. Died 23 November 1942
17th Aero Squadron
6 victories

1st Lieutenant Robert Opie Lindsay
DSC
From Madison, North Carolina, born 25 December 1894. Died 1 August 1952
139th Aero Squadron USAS
6 victories

1st Lieutenant John K MacArthur
DSC
From Everett, Washington DC, born Columbia, PA. Killed France, 20 July 1918
27th Aero Squadron USAS
6 victories

Major David McKelvey Peterson
DSC* LdH(F) CdG(F)
From Honesdale, Pennsylvania, born 2 July 1895. KIFA Daytona Beach, Florida, 16 March 1919
N124 Escadrille, 103rd, 94th & 95th Aero Sqns USAS
6 victories
(Peterson stands by a Nieuport 28)

Lieutenant Cleo Francis Pineau
DFC
From Albuquerque, New Mexico, born 23 July 1893. Died Williamsport, Pennsylvania, May 1972
210 Squadron RAF
6 victories

1st Lieutenant William Thomas Ponder
DSC CdG(F)
Born Llano, Texas, 26 March 1893. Died Amarillo, Texas, 27 February 1947
Spa 67 & Spa163 Escdrilles, 103rd Aero Sqn USAS
6 victories
(In the picture Ponder is standing in front of a Spad)

Captain Bogart Rogers
Born Los Angeles, CA, 24 June 1898. Died Burbank, CA, 24 July 1966
32 Squadron RAF
6 victories

1st Lieutenant William Howard Stovall
DSC
From Stovall, Mississippi, born 18 February 1895. Died Stovall, 11 May 1970
13th Aero Squadron USAS
6 victories

1st Lieutenant Edgar Gardner Tobin
DSC
From San Antonio, Texas, born 1895. KIFA Lake Wallace, Louisiana, 10 January 1954
103rd Aero Squadron USAS
6 victories

Captain Jerry Cox Vasconcells
CdG(F)
Born Lyons, Kansas, 3 December 1892. Died Denver, Colorado, 17 April 1950
27th & 185th Aero Squadrons USAS
6 victories

1st Lieutenant Remington deB Vernam
DSC
From New York, NY, born 24 March 1896. DoW France, 1 December 1918
Spa96 Escadrille, 22nd Aero Sqn USAS
6 victories

1st Lieutenant Joseph Fritz Wehner
DSC*
Born Boston, Massachusetts, born 20 September 1895. KIA France, 18 September 1918
186th Aero Squadron, 27th Aero Squadron USAS
6 victories

Lieutenant Howard Koch Boysen
Italian Silver Medal
Born in 1892, he came from either Dallas, Texas, or Chicago, Illinois.
66 Squadron RAF
5 victories
(Boysen is on the left, with A. Koch of 70 Sqn RAF (10))

Lieutenant Sydney MacGillvary Brown
DFC
Born Brooklyn, New York, born 10 August 1895. Died Pittsburgh, PA, 7 April 1952
29 Squadron RAF
5 victories
(Brown is standing in front of a Sopwith Dolphin)

Captain Harold Robert Buckley
DSC* CdG(F)
Born Westfield, Massachusetts, born 4 April 1896. Died Rigby, Idaho, 13 June 1958
American Field Ambulance Service, 95th Aero Squadron USAS
5 victories

1st Lieutenant Lawrence Kingsley Callahan
DFC
Born Louisville, Kentucky, 11 January 1894. Died Gardena, California, 17 September 1977
85 Sqn RAF, 148th Aero Sqn USAS
5 victories

Captain Charles Rudolph D'Olive
DSC
Born Sugarville, Alabama, 10 July 1896. Died Waterloo, Iowa, 20 July 1974
93rd and 141st Aero Squadrons USAS
5 victories
(D'Olive is on the left, with Capt H. Baker, 141st Aero)

1st Lieutenant George Willard Furlow
DSC*
Born Rochester, Minnesota, 24 March 1893. Died November 1959
103rd Aero Squadron USAS
5 victories

1st Lieutenant Harold Huston George
DSC
Born Lockport, New York, 19 July 1893. KOAS Darwin, Australia, 30 April 1942
139th Aero Squadron USAS
5 victories
(In the picture George is in front of a DH4)

Captain Charles Gossage Grey
DSC
From Chicago, Illinois, born 20 June 1894. Died Palm Beach, California, 1984+
Spa93 Escadrille, 213rd Aero Sqn USAS
5 victories
(+ victim of a hit-and-run auto accident)

1st Lieutenant Edward M Haight
From Astoria, New York, born 30 May 1896. Died St. Petersburg, Florida, 5 December 1975
139th Aero Squadron USAS
5 victories

1st Lieutenant James Knowles Jr
DSC CdG(F)
Born Cincinnati, Ohio, born 27 December 1896. Died St Louis, Missouri, 21 February 1971
95th Aero Squadron USAS
5 victories

1st Lieutenant Frederick Ernest Luff
DFC
From Cleveland, Ohio, born 9 July 1896. Died Cleveland, 27 April 1931
74 Sqn RAF, 25th Aero USAS
5 victories

Lieutenant Francis Peabody Magoun
MC
Born New York City, NY, 6 January 1895. Died Cambridge, Massachusetts, 5 June 1979
U.S. Ambulance Service; 1 Squadron RAF
5 victories

1st Lieutenant Zenos Ramsey Miller
Born Pao Ting Fu, China, 13 September 1895. KIFA Framlingham, Mass., 22 July 1922
27th Aero Squadron USAS
5 victories

1st Lieutenant Ralph Ambrose O'Neill
DSC** Bronze Star CdG(F)
Born San Francisco, CA, 7 December 1898. Died Redwood City, California, 23 December 1980
147th Aero Squadron USAS
5 victories

2nd Lieutenant John Sidney Owens
Born Philadelphia, PA, 26 May 1898. Died Coral Gables, Florida, 14 January 1965
139th Aero Squadron
5 victories

2nd Lieutenant Kenneth Lee Porter
DSC CdG(F)
From Dowagiac, Michigan, 6 December 1896. Died Jackson Heights, NY, 3 February 1988
147th Aero Squadron USAS
5 victories

1st Lieutenant Orville Alfred Ralston
DSC
From Lincoln, Nebraska, born 19 November 1897. Died May 1970
85 Sqn RAF, 148th Aero Sqn USAS
5 victories

1st Lieutenant John J Seerley
Born Burlington, Iowa, 21 November 1897. Died Tetsworth, Oxfordshire, England, 21 August 1943
13th Aero Squadron USAS
5 victories

1st Lieutenant Harold Goodman Shoemaker
KIFA, France, 6 October 1918
74 Sqn RAF, 17th Aero Sqn USAS
5 victories

1st Lieutenant Francis M Simonds Jr
Born Flushing, NY, 17 October 1894. Died Naples, Florida, 10 July 1961
147th Aero Squadron
5 victories

Lieutenant Edgar Taylor
From Central Falls, Long Island, NY, born 1897. KIA France, 24 August 1918
79 Squadron RAF
5 victories

Lieutenant-Colonel William Thaw
DSC* LdH(F) MM(F) CdG(F)
From Pittsburgh, Pennsylvania, 12 August 1893. Died Pittsburgh, 22 April 1934
D6, C42, N65 & N124 Escadrilles, 103rd Aero Sqn, & 3rd PG USAS
5 victories

1st Lieutenant William Duncan Tipton
Born Tarretsville, Maryland, 11 December 1892. KIFA Adena, Ohio, 12 December 1945
3 Sqn RAF, 17th Aero Sqn USAS
5 victories

Lieutenant George Donald Tod
Born 15 January 1898
65 Squadron RAF
5 victories

1st Lieutenant Robert Miles Todd
From Cincinnati, Ohio, born 24 June 1897. Died La Jalla, California, 20 Janury 1988
17th Aero Squadron USAS
5 victories

Lieutenant Eugene Seeley Coler (NO PHOTO)
DFC
From Newark, New Jersey, born 13 January 1896.
DOAS Gerrard's Cross, England, 30 August 1953
11 Squadron RAF
16 victories

Lieutenant Archibald Buchanan (NO PHOTO)
DFC
Born Long Island, NY, 5 October 1892.
210 Squadron RAF
7 victories

1st Lieutenant James A Healey (NO PHOTO)
DSC CdG(F)
Born Kansas, Missouri, born 26 March 1895. Died Fort Worth, Texas, 8 May 1983
147th Aero Squadron USAS
5 victories

Lieutenant Malcolm Clifford Howell (NO PHOTO)
From Boonton, New Jersey, born 1 December 1895. Died Westminster, NY, June 1976
208 Squadron RAF
5 victories

1st Lieutenant Donald Frederick Murmann (NO PHOTO)
Born 14 November 1898
40 Sqn RAF; 25th US Aero Sqn
5 victories

2nd Lieutenant Osborne John Orr (NO PHOTO)
DFC
Born Cleveland, Ohio, 15 July, 1895. KIA France, 23 October 1918
204 Squadron RAF
5 victories

British Aces in Alphabetical Order

Name	Victories
Alberry, F	7
Aldred, J W	8
Aldridge, J A	5
Alexander, W M	22
Allen, C P	7
Amm, E O	10
Anderson, G B	5
Anderson, G F	8
Andrews, J O	12
Apps, G F M	10
Armstrong, D'U V	5
Armstrong, F C	13
Arnison, C H	9
Arnold, A R	5
Aspinall, J V	6
Atkey, A C	38
Atkinson, E D	10
Babbage, F F	5
Bailey, G G	8
Baker, B E	12
Baker, L D	5
Baker, T C R	12
Baldwin, O M	16
Balfour, H H	9
Ball, A	44
Banbury,F E	11
Banks, C C	13
Bannerman, R B	17
Barkell, T H	7
Barker, W G	50
Barlow, J L	6
Barlow, L M	20
Barton, H D	19
Bateman, J C	7
Bawlf, L D	5
Beamish, H F	11
Beanlands, B P H	8
Beard, D W	8
Beauchamp-Proctor, A W	54
Beaver, W	19
Beck, A	11
Beddow, H H	10
Belgrave, J D	18
Bell, C G	5
Bell, D J	20
Bell, G G	16
Bell, H B	10
Bell-Irving, A D	7
Benbow, E L	8
Bennett, R G	9
Bennett, R M	5
Berlyn, R C	5
Billinge, F	5
Binnie, J A W	9
Birkbeck, R A	10
Birks, G A	12
Bishop, A W	72
Biziou, H A R	8
Blake, A W	5
Bland, W H	7
Blaxland, G H	8
Blenkiron, A V	5
Boger, W O	5
Bond, W A	5
Booker, C D	29
Booth, E B	5
Bott, A J	5
Boulton, N S	6
Boulton, P	6
Bowles, F S	5
Bowman, G H	32
Brading, R C B	13
Brand, C J Q	12
Breadner, L S	10
Breakey, J D	9
Bremridge, G	5
Brewster-Joske, C A	8
Bridgeman, O C	5
Britnall, F J S	9
Broadberry, E W	8
Brock, C G	6
Bromley, E C	12
Brookes, E G	6
Brown, A J	8
Brown, A R	5
Brown, A R	10
Brown, C P	14
Brown, F E	10
Brown, W H	9
Brownell, R J	12
Bryson, O C	12
Bulmer, G W	9
Burden, H J	16
Burge, P S	11
Burger, M G S	5
Bush, J C	6
Byrne, P A	10
Cairnes, W J	6
Caldwell, K L	25
Callaghan, J C	5
Cameron, D E	5
Campbell, L	7
Campbell, W C	24
Candy, J G S	6
Capel, L H T	7
Carlaw, W Mac	12
Carlin, S	10
Carpenter, P	24
Carter, A D	28
Carter, A W	17
Casey, F D	9
Chadwick, A J	11
Chandler, R N	7
Chapman, C M B	7
Chappell, R W	11
Charley, R M	5
Chick, J S	16
Chidlaw-Roberts, R L	10
Child, J E	5
Child, J M	8
Chisam, W H	7
Clappison, H G	6
Clark, A G	5
Clark, C C	10
Clarke, E D	6
Claxton, W G	37
Claydon, A	7
Clayson, P J	29
Clear, E A	12
Clement, C M	14
Clements, H G	6
Coath, R D	9
Cobby, A H	29
Cochrane-Patrick, W	21
Cock, G H	13
Cockerell, S	7
Colbert, J H	6
Cole, A T	9
Cole, E S T	8
Collett, C F	11
Collishaw, R	61
Colvill-Jones, T	11
Compston, R J O	25
Compton, H N	6
Conder, R E	6
Coningham, A	14
Conn, K B	20
Cooke, D G	13
Coombe, J G	8
Coombes, L P	15
Cooper, A G	7
Cooper, G K	6
Cooper, M L	6
Cottle, J	13
Cowan, S E	7
Cowell, J J	16
Cowper, A K	19
Cox, G J	5
Cox, G M	5
Crabb, E F	6
Craig, W B	8
Crawford, K	5
Crole, G B	5
Crompton, J B	5
Crowe, C M	15
Crundall, E D	7
Cudemore, C W	15
Cullen, R J	5
Culling, T G	6
Cummings, E D	9
Cummings, L	5
Cunnell, D C	9
Cunningham, J A	10
Cunninghame, F J	5
Cunningham-Reid, A S	7
Curphy, W G S	6
Curtis, R L	15
Curtis, W A	13
Dallas, R S	32
Dalrymple, S	5
Daly, J E A R	6
Daly, R H	7
Daniel, H C	9
Darwin, C J W	5
Davey, H B	6
Davidson, C R	6
Davies, D A	10
Davies, E E	7
Davies, E G	10
Davies, F J	12
Davis, E F H	7
Davison, H F	11
Dawe, J J	8
Dawes, R J	9
Day, H	11
Day, M J G	5
De Pencier, J D	8
De Roeper, B P H	5
Debenham. H G W	6
DeFontenay, P A	5
Del'Haye, R A	9
Dennett, P M	7
Dewhirst, J H	7
Dickson, E	14
Dixon, G C	9
Dodds, R	10

Dolan, H E 7
Doran, T A 7
Doyle, J E 9
Drake, E B 5
Draper, C 9
Drewitt, H F S 7
Drinkwater, A T 9
Drummond, J E 6
Drummond, R M 8
Duffus, C S 5
Duncan, G M 8
Duncan, W J A 11
Durrand, W 8
Durrant, T 11
Eaton, E C 5
Edwards, C G 7
Edwards, H J 5
Edwards, S T 17
Elliott, H W 5
Ellis, H E O 7
Ellis, S E 5
Ellwood, A B 10
Elton, E J 16
Enstone, A J 13
Evans, H C 5
Eycott-Martin, H R 8
Eyre, C A 6
Fairclough, A B 19
Falkenberg, C F 17
Fall, J S T 36
Farquhar, R W 7
Farrell, C McA G 7
Farrow, W H 10
Fielding-Johnson, W S 6
Findlay, C 14
Findlay, J P 6
Findlay, M H 14
Firth, J C B 11
Fitzgibbon, D F 9
Fitz-Morris, J 15
Fleming, A L 8
Foot, E L 5
Forman, J H 9
Forrest, H G 11
Foster, G B 7
Foster, R M 16
Fowler, H H S 5
Franklyn, A W 6
Freehill, M M 7
Frew, M B 23
Fry, W M 11
Fullard, P F 40
Galbraith, D M B 6
Gardiner, G C 6
Gardner, C V 10
Gates, G B 16
Gauld, G W G 5
Gerrard, T F N 10
Gibbons, F G 14
Gibbons, G E 17
Gibbs, F J 11
Gibbs, G E 10
Gifford, R C D'A 6
Gilbertson, D H S 5
Giles, W B 5
Gillespie, W J 5
Gilmour, J I 39
Glen, J A 15
Glynn, C B 8
Goble, S J 10
Godfrey, A E 14
Gonne, M E 5
Good, H B 5
Goode, H K 15
Goodison, H A F 5
Gordon, F S 9
Gordon, R M 9
Gorringe, F C 14
Gopsill, K L 5
Gossip, G H D 6
Goulding, A G 9
Graham, G L 13
Graham, R 5
Grange, E R 5
Gray, W E 5
Green, C D B 11
Green, J H R 5
Green, W B 7
Greene, J E 15
Grenfell, E O 8
Gribben, E 5
Grinnell-Milne, D W 6
Groom, V E 8
Grosvenor, R A 16
Gurdon, J E 28
Hackwill, G H 9
Haines, A J 6
Hales, J P 6
Hall, F V 7
Hall, R N 6
Hallonquist, J E 5
Hamersley, H A 13
Hamilton, H J 6
Hamilton. L 6
Hammersley, R G 8
Hand, E McN 5
Hardman, J D I 9
Harlock, F G 8
Harries, T M 11
Harris, A T 5
Harrison, T S 22
Harrison, W L 12
Hartley, H H 7
Harvey, W F J 26
Hawker, L G 7
Hay, H A 5
Hay, R B 5
Hayne, E T 15
Hazell, T F 43
Headlam, E S 5
Hegarty, H G 8
Hemming, A S 8
Hemming, G W 6
Henderson, I H D 7
Hepburn, A 16
Heron, O A P 13
Hewat, R A 6
Hickey, C R R 21
Hicks, G R 8
Highwood, S W 16
Hilborn, W C 7
Hinchcliffe, W G R 6
Hind, I F 8
Hobson, F 15
Hobson, P K 7
Hodson, G S 10
Hoidge, R T C 28
Holliday, F P 17
Hollinghurst, L N 11
Hooper, G H 11
Horn, S B 13
Horry, T S 8
Howard, R W 8
Howe, P F C 5
Howell, C E 19
Howsom, G R 13
Hoy, E C 13
Hubbard, W 10
Hubbard, W H 12
Hudson, F H 6
Hudson, H B 13
Hughes, D J 5
Hughes, E Y 5
Hughes, G F 11
Hunt, F J 9
Hunter, J E L 12
Hunter, T V 6
Hurst, C E 5
Huskinson, P 11
Hustings, N W 7
Huston, V H 6
Hyde, G A 5
Irving, G B 12
Irwin, W R 11
James, M R 11
Jarvis, A E DeM 7
Jarvis, A G 5
Jarvis, L W 7
Jeffs, C H 5
Jenkin, L F 22
Jenkins, W E 10
Jenkins, W S 12
Jerrard, A 7
Johns, R L 9
Johnson, F 16
Johnson, G O 11
Johnston, E C 20
Johnston, P A 6
Johnstone, E G 17
Jones, A L 7
Jones, G 7
Jones, H W G 7
Jones, J I T 37
Jones, N C 9
Jones-Williams, A G 11
Jordan, W L 39
Joseph, S C 13
Joslyn, H W 7
Junor, K W 8
Keeble, N 6
Keen, A W 14
Keirstead, R McN 13
Kelly, E T S 6
Kenney, E P 7
Kerby, H S 9
Kiddie, A C 15
King, C F 22
King, E R 26
King, L W 9
Kinkead, S M 35
Kirkman, R K 8
Kitto, F M 9
Knight, A G 8
Koch, A 10
Kullberg, H A 19
Lagesse, C H R 20
Laing, K J P 5
Lale, H P 23

Langlands, D ... 5
Larkin, H J ... 11
Latimer, D ... 28
Latta, J D ... 5
Laurence, F H ... 5
Lavers, C S I ... 9
Lawson, G E B ... 6
Leacroft, J ... 22
Leask, K M StC G ... 8
LeBlanc-Smith, M ... 6
Lee, A S G ... 7
Leitch, A A ... 7
Leith, J L ... 9
Lennox, J S ... 5
Letts, J H T ... 13
Lewis, C A ... 8
Lewis, G H ... 12
Lightbody, J D ... 5
Lindup, E ... 5
Lingham, G A ... 6
Little, R A ... 47
Little, R H ... 5
Liversedge, S T ... 13
Lloyd, G L ... 8
Lloyd-Evans, D ... 8
Long, S H ... 9
Longton, W H ... 11
Lowe, C N ... 9
Loyd, A T ... 6
Luchford, H G E ... 24
Luke, T C ... 6
MacAndrew, C G O ... 5
MacDonald, H O ... 7
MacDonald, R M ... 5
MacDonald, W M ... 8
MacGregor, N M ... 7
MacKay, G C ... 18
Mackereth, J ... 7
MacLaren, D R ... 54
Maclanachan, W ... 7
MacLean, L J ... 5
MacLeod, M P ... 7
Macmillan, N ... 9
MacRae, J F N ... 5
Maddocks, H H ... 7
Makepeace, R M ... 17
Malcolm, R G ... 8
Malley, G F ... 6
Malone, J J ... 10
Manley, P S ... 5
Mann, W E G ... 13
Mannock, E ... 73
Mansbridge, L M ... 5
Mansell, W S ... 5
Manuel, J G ... 13
Manuel, R L ... 12
Manzer, R ... 11
Marchant, C J ... 9
Mare-Montembault, M J J G ... 6
Mark, R T ... 14
Marks, G I D ... 8
Martin, W T ... 6
Masters, E H ... 8
Maud, C M ... 11
Mauduit, R F S ... 9
Maund, H B ... 8
Mawle, N W R ... 12
Maxted, W S ... 5
Maxwell, G J C ... 26
Maxwell, R S ... 9
May, W R ... 13
Maybery, R A ... 21
Maynard, F H M ... 6
McCall, F R G ... 35
McCall, M ... 6
McClintock, R StC ... 5
McCloughry, E J K ... 21
McConnell, R K ... 7
McCudden, J A ... 8
McCudden, J T B ... 57
McDonald, I D R ... 20
McDonald, J S ... 9
McDonald, R ... 8
McDougall, P A ... 7
McElroy, G E H ... 46
McEvoy, C ... 9
McEwen, C M ... 27
McGinness, P J ... 7
McGoun, D M ... 9
McGregor, D U ... 12
McGregor, M C ... 11
McKay, A E ... 10
McKeever, A E ... 31
McKenzie, R W ... 6
McLaughlin, R ... 6
McMaking, O L ... 6
McNearney, J H ... 5
McQuiston, F ... 10
McRae, R F ... 5
Mealing, M E ... 14
Medlicott, H W ... 5
Meek, E S ... 6
Meggitt, G W ... 6
Meintjes, H ... 8
Mellersh, F J W ... 5
Mellings, H T ... 15
Middleton, T P ... 28
Miller, A W B ... 6
Millman, N C ... 6
Mills, K C ... 5
Milne, J T ... 9
Minifie, R P ... 21
Mitchell, J H ... 11
Molesworth, W E ... 18
Molyneaux, H A S ... 5
Montgomery, K B ... 12
Moody, B H ... 9
Moody, H M ... 8
Moore, G B ... 10
Morgan, J T ... 5
Morrow, E T ... 7
Mostyn, W J ... 5
Mott, H E ... 5
Mulock, R H ... 5
Munday, R B ... 9
Murlis-Green, G W ... 8
Muspratt, K K ... 8
Nangle, H C M ... 5
Napier, C G D ... 9
Napier, I P R ... 12
Nash, G E ... 6
Nash, T W ... 8
Nel, W J B ... 7
Neville, R H G ... 5
Newnham, M A ... 18
Newsome, T H ... 5
Norton, E W ... 9
O'Grady, S C ... 9
Oades, S A ... 11
Oaks, H A ... 11
Odell, C W ... 7
Oliver, T A ... 5
Olivier, E ... 8
Olley, G P ... 10
Orlebar, A H ... 7
Owen, E E ... 5
Owen, R J ... 7
Page, J A ... 7
Paget, A ... 6
Palliser, A J ... 7
Park, K R ... 20
Pashley, E C ... 8
Patey, H A ... 11
Patrick, W D ... 7
Paul, C S ... 5
Payne, J D ... 14
Payne, L A ... 11
Paynter, J deC ... 10
Payton, C W ... 11
Pearson, W R G ... 7
Peck, A H ... 8
Pennell, E R ... 5
Pentland, A A N D ... 23
Peters, G C ... 7
Peverell, E H ... 5
Phillipps, R C ... 15
Pickthorn, C E M ... 5
Pidcock, G A H ... 6
Pierce, E ... 9
Pilditch, G ... 5
Pinder, J W ... 17
Poole, G R ... 5
Pope, S L G ... 6
Powell, F J ... 5
Pratt, H J ... 5
Pratt, S H ... 7
Preston, J C ... 7
Price, FC G W ... 12
Price, S W ... 7
Price, W T ... 7
Pritt, W A ... 6
Prothero, P B ... 8
Puffer, S A ... 7
Purdom, T L ... 13
Quested, J B ... 8
Quigley, F G ... 33
Rae, T G ... 6
Ralston, J S ... 12
Randall, A C ... 10
Randall, G E ... 11
Ransley, F C ... 9
Rath, H C ... 12
Ray, L H ... 7
Raymond-Barker, R ... 6
Rayner, J W ... 5
Redgate, O W ... 16
Redler, H B ... 10
Reed, A E ... 19
Reed, W E ... 9
Rees, L W B ... 8
Reeves, H G ... 13
Reid, E V ... 19
Reid, G R M ... 9
Reid, G P S ... 5
Rhys Davids, A P F ... 25
Rice-Oxley, A ... 6
Richards, C R ... 11
Richardson, H B ... 15

Richardson, L L ... 7
Ridley, C B ... 11
Rigby, H A ... 6
Riley, A I ... 5
Riley, G R ... 13
Robb, J M ... 7
Roberts, N ... 5
Robinson, H N C ... 10
Rochford, L H ... 29
Rogers, W W ... 9
Rooper, W T V ... 8
Rose, T ... 11
Rosevear, S W ... 25
Ross, C G ... 20
Rowley, H V ... 9
Roxburgh-Smith, B ... 22
Roy, I L ... 10
Rusby, R H ... 10
Rutherford, W J ... 8
Saint, H J T ... 7
Salter, E J ... 9
Sanday, W D S ... 5
Sanderson, I C ... 11
Satchell,H L ... 8
Saundby, R H M S ... 5
Saunders, A W ... 12
Saunders, F G ... 8
Saunders, H W L ... 15
Savage, D A ... 7
Sawyer, C H ... 8
Scandrett, H ... 7
Scholte, O F J ... 8
Scott, A J L ... 5
Scott, M D G ... 12
Seabrook, J P ... 5
Sellars, H W ... 8
Seth-Smith, K G ... 7
Sharman, J E ... 8
Sharpe, F ... 5
Sharpe, T S ... 6
Shepherd, A S ... 10
Shields, W E ... 24
Shook, A MacD ... 12
Siddall, J H ... 9
Sidebottom, W ... 14
Simonson, E L ... 5
Simpson, G G ... 8
Sims, C J ... 9
Slater, J A ... 24
Slatter, L H ... 7
Sloley, R H ... 9
Smart, W A ... 5
Smith, D E ... 6
Smith, E A L F ... 7
Smith, F R ... 16
Smith, H C ... 5
Smith, J H ... 8
Smith, R M ... 11
Smith, S P ... 5
Smith-Grant, J G S C ... 5
Smuts, N R ... 5
Smythe, C R ... 6
Sneath, W H ... 5
Soar, R R ... 12
Soden, F O ... 27
Solly, A N ... 9
Sorsoleil, J V ... 14
Southey, W A ... 20
Sowrey, F ... 13
Spence, A G A ... 9
Stackard, H F ... 15
Stanger, S ... 13
Stanton, F C ... 7
Staton, W E ... 26
Stead, I O ... 5
Steele, C R ... 7
Stephens, E J ... 13
Stephenson, T F ... 5
Stephenson, W S ... 12
Stevens, F D ... 5
Stewart, D A ... 16
Stewart, O ... 5
Stone, C O ... 7
Strange, G J ... 7
Strugnell, W V ... 6
Stuart-Wortley, R N M ... 6
Stubbs, C L ... 7
Summers, J K ... 8
Sutton, O M ... 7
Swale, E ... 17
Swayze, W K ... 6
Sykes, R ... 6
Symondson, F S ... 13
Symons, H L ... 6
Taplin, L T E ... 12
Tayler, StC C ... 10
Taylor, A G V ... 7
Taylor, F H ... 10
Taylor, G P ... 6
Taylor, M S ... 7
Tempest, E R ... 17
Thayre, F J H ... 20
Thomas, M ... 5
Thompson, C R ... 6
Thompson, C R J ... 6
Thompson, C W McK ... 12
Thompson, S F H ... 30
Thomson, G E ... 21
Thomson, W McK ... 26
Thornely, R R ... 10
Tidmarsh, D M ... 7
Todd, J ... 18
Tonkin, A V ... 6
Tonks, A J B ... 12
Traill, T C ... 8
Trapp, G L ... 6
Travers, F D ... 9
Travers, H G ... 5
Trescowthick, N C ... 7
Trevethan, R M ... 12
Trollope, J L ... 18
Tudhope, J H ... 10
Tudhope, P M ... 6
Turnbull, J S ... 5
Turner, A H ... 5
Tyrell, W A ... 18
Unger, K R ... 14
Vaucour, A M ... 7
Venter, C J ... 16
Vickers, O H D ... 13
Vigers, A W ... 14
Vlasto, A G ... 8
Walker, K M ... 5
Walkerdine, B A ... 6
Walkerdine, H J ... 7
Wallace, H LeR ... 14
Wallage, S H ... 10
Wallwork, J W ... 5
Walter, S R P ... 7
Wareing, G W ... 9
Warner, J W ... 8
Watson, H E ... 6
Watson, H G ... 14
Watson, K B ... 9
Weare, F G C ... 15
Webb, N W W ... 14
Wells, W L ... 10
Wellwood, J J ... 7
Welsh, G A ... 5
West, M S ... 5
Weston, D J ... 13
Westwood, W G ... 6
Whealy, A T ... 27
Wheeler, W A ... 6
Whistler, H A ... 23
White, H G ... 7
White, J B ... 12
White, J L M ... 22
Whitehead, L E ... 5
Whitney, R K ... 5
Wilkinson, A M ... 19
Williams, E G H C ... 5
Williams, F J ... 5
Williams, T F ... 14
Williams, T M ... 9
Williamson, A ... 9
Wilson, C F C ... 5
Wilson, C M ... 8
Wilson, P ... 7
Winkler, W O B ... 6
Winnicott, R ... 10
Winter, R R ... 5
Womersley, J H G ... 5
Wood, A W ... 11
Wood, H A ... 5
Wood, W B ... 13
Woollett, H W ... 35
Woollven, C H C ... 5
Worthington, C E ... 5
Wright, W A ... 8
Yeates, V M ... 8
Young, G C ... 5
Young, W E ... 11
Zink, E L ... 5

American Aces in alphabetical order

Baer, P F ... 9
Bair, H L ... 6
Baylies, F L ... 12
Beane, J D ... 6
Bennett Jr, L ... 12
Biddle, C J ... 7
Bissell, C L ... 6
Bissonette, C A ... 6
Boyson, H K ... 5
Brooks, A R ... 6
Brown, S MacG ... 5
Buchanan, A ... 7
Buckley, H R ... 5
Burdick, H ... 8
Callahan, L K ... 5
Callender, A A ... 8
Campbell, D ... 6
Cassady, T G ... 9
Catto, C G ... 6
Chambers, R McK ... 7

Clay Jr, H R 8
Coler, E S 16
Connelly Jr, J A 7
Cook, H W 7
Coolidge, H 8
Cooper, N 6
Creech, J O 7
Curtis, E P 6
D'Olive, C R 5
Donaldson, J O 7
Furlow, G W 5
George, H H 5
Grey, C G 5
Guthrie, M K 6
Griffiths, J S 7
Haight, E M 5
Hale, F L 7
Hamilton, L A 10
Hartney, H E 7
Hays, F K 6
Healy, J A 5
Hilton, D'A F 8
Holden Jr, L C 7
Howell, M C 5
Hudson, D 6
Hunter, F O'D 9
Iaccaci, A T 17
Iaccaci, P T 17
Ingalls, D S 6
Jones Jr, C S 8
Kindley, F E 12
Knight, D 10
Knotts, H C 6
Knowles Jr, J 5
Kullberg, H A 19
Lambert, W C 18
Landis, R G 12
Larner, G deF 7
LeBoutillier, O C 10
Libby, F 14
Lindsay, R O 6
Lord, F I 12
Lufbery, G R 16
Luff, F E 5
Luke Jr, F 18
Lussier, E J 11
Magoun, F P 5
MacArthur, J K 6
Meissner, J A 8
Miller, Z R 5
Murmann, D F 5
O'Neill, R A 5
Orr, O J 5
Owens, J S 5
Parsons, E C 8
Pearson, J W 11
Peterson, D McK 6
Pineau, C F 6
Ponder, W T 6
Porter, K L 5
Putnam, D E 13
Ralston, O A 5
Rickenbacker, E V 26
Robertson, W A 7
Rogers, B 6
Rose, O J 16
Rummell, L J 7
Schoen Jr, K 7
Seerley, J J 5
Sewell, S 7
Shoemaker, H G 5
Simon, W K 8
Simonds Jr, F M 5
Springs, E W 16
Stenseth, M 8
Stovell, W H 6
Swaab, J M 10
Taylor, E 5
Thaw, W 5
Tipton, W D 5
Tobin, E G 6
Tod, G O 5
Todd, R M 5
Unger, K R 14
Vasconcells, J C 6
Vaughan Jr, G A 13
Vernam, R deB 6
Warman, C W 12
Wehner, J F 6
White, H A 7
White Jr, W W 8
Wright, C E 9

Also from the Publisher

BRITISH AVIATION SQUADRON MARKINGS

of World War I: RFC • RAF • RNAS

Les Rogers

Years in the making, this book covers the wide variety of markings used by British aviation units in World War I. Organized numerically by squadron number the book includes both textual and photographic examples for nearly all RFC, RAF, and RNAS squadrons. Many of the photographs are published here for the first time, and the color profiles offer a representative selection of units, aircraft, and color schemes. A classic book.

Size: 9"x12" • over 800 b/w photographs, 150 color aircraft profiles • 296 pp.
ISBN: 0-7643-1284-7 • hard cover • $69.95

ITALIAN ACES OF WORLD WAR I

and their Aircraft

Roberto Gentilli, Antonio Iozzi & Paolo Varriale

For the first time, a detailed history of a little known aspect of the Great War in the air: the forty-two Italian aces. From legendary personalities such as Francesco Baracca and Scaroni to completely forgotten aces, each biography details their personalities, and their combat careers during and after the war. Charts report all their victories, with careful cross-referencing to Austrian and German losses. An introduction puts the air war on the Italian front in perspective, showing the development and actions of the Italian air force including many orders of battle, and brief histories of all fighter squadrons. Over 500 previously unpublished photographs from private sources, as well as twenty-four pages of color profiles of Nieuports, Spads, Hanriots and Macchis provide a stunning visual complement for the historian and modeler.

Size: 9"x12" • over 500 black and white photos and color aircraft profiles • 496 pp.
ISBN: 0-7643-1664-8 • hard cover • $69.95

THE CAMEL DRIVERS

The 17th Aero Squadron in World War I

Otis Lowell Reed & George Roland

The 17th Aero Squadron flew Sopwith Camels under British command along the Western Front during the summer of 1918. This definitive work on the 17th Aero Squadron in World War I is drawn from a wide range of official and personal sources, including original squadron records (found in an attic!), numerous interviews, letters written home, and half a dozen diaries – including one kept by a German pilot flying in opposition.

Size: 8 1/2"x11" • over 200 b/w photographs • 160 pp.
ISBN: 0-7643-0071-7 • hardcover • $45.00

THE HAT IN THE RING GANG

The Combat History of the 94th Aero Squadron in World War I

Charles Woolley

This all new book contains a rich mixture of official as well as personal contemporarily written accounts of the 94th Aero Squadron, the most successful pursuit squadron in the United States Air Service. Combat reports, letters of the aces, and diary entries of other pilots are woven together to tell the story. Rosters of pilots, aircraft, and citations for bravery awards round out this lively history of war in the air, spotlighting the gallant 94th.

Size: 8 1/2"x11" • 375 b/w photographs, color profiles • 272 pp.
ISBN: 0-7643-1427-0 • hard cover • $49.95

FIRST TO THE FRONT

The Aerial Adventures of 1st Lt. Waldo Heinrichs and the 95th Aero Squadron 1917-1918

Charles Woolley

The 95th Aero Squadron was the first American pursuit squadron to fly over the front in March 1918 and 1st Lt. Waldo Heinrichs was one of its original members. Told through the words of those who served, Heinrichs' richly written diary forms the nucleus of the story supported by contemporary letters, anecdotes, and combat reports from many of the other flyers. Photos, most unpublished from the personal albums of the participants, show planes, places and personnel.

Size: 8 1/2"x11" • 280 b/w photographs, color profiles • 240 pp.
ISBN: 0-7643-0749-5 • hard cover • $49.95

THE LAFAYETTE FLYING CORPS

The American Volunteers in the French Air Service in World War I

Dennis Gordon

Includes detailed biographies of the 269 volunteer American airmen and gunners of France's Service Aeronautique who flew in sixty-six pursuit and twenty-seven bomber/observation squadrons over the Western Front – also included are the thirty-eight pilots of the Escadrille Lafayette. It is an accurate and absorbing account of the lives and combat experiences of the men who later formed the nucleus of the American Expeditionary Force squadrons. Contains comprehensive research, including details of war casualties and survivors, and many unpublished photographs.

Size: 8 1/2"x11" • over 320 and b/w photographs • 504 pp.
ISBN: 0-7643-1108-5 • hard cover • $59.95